The Elie and Earlsferry History Society wishes to thank the following organisations whose generous grants have assisted the Society in the publication of this history of our area.

Awards for All
Elie & Earlsferry Improvements Association
Elie Fayre Day Group
Elie Harbour Trust
Fife Council
The Strathmartine Trust

D1638858   Bell
man

For Ian Rookie
With best wishes
Archie Rennie

THE HARBOURS OF ELIE BAY

A HISTORY

ARCHIE RENNIE

ELIE AND EARLSFERRY HISTORY SOCIETY

Printed and bound in Aberdeen by XIC

Published by Elie and Earlsferry History Society

ISBN 978-0-9557944-0-7

Contents

Preface

The harbours of Elie Bay have been of service for many centuries. This history traces their development and use from the earliest times to 1975. It sets the varying roles of the harbours over the centuries in the context of relevant local and national and sometimes international developments, to show how even minor harbours in a small community can have a part to play in these larger affairs, as well as how events in the wider world greatly affected how the harbours were developed and used.

The sources which I have used are listed at the end. Much of what I have written is based on published sources; but much has also come from unpublished documents, mainly a substantial archive of local material collected by David Thomson, Elie Estate papers and other documents in the National Archives of Scotland, and documents in the care of the University of St. Andrews.

I regret that this is not a properly-referenced history; but my untrained working methods and record-keeping were too disorderly to make that possible. Not all my sources can be regarded as equally reliable; but I have drawn upon the best authorities I could find and have found nothing in extensive reading to contradict the accounts on which I have relied. Where it has seemed justifiable to make a conjecture I have tried in the language I use to indicate this. In my acknowledgements I have tried to show how much I owe to the generous helpers who have made this work possible. Any errors are my own.

Acknowledgements

In the preparation of this work I have had a great deal of help from many people in Elie and elsewhere.

I and the Society wish to thank the following for permission to use pictures: St. Andrews University Library for No. 14 and 27; the National Maritime Museum for No. 9; David and Charles (Publishers) Ltd for No. 19; Jimmy Linton for Nos. 1, 7, 20, 22, 24, 25, 26, 27, 29 and 32; Alan Provan for Nos. 2, 3, 18 and 23; Colin Martin for No. 6; and the National Library of Scotland for permission to reproduce an extract from the 6-inch Ordnance Survey Map of 1854.

I particularly wish to thank the members of staff of St. Andrews University Library and of the National Archives of Scotland, who have produced for me many original documents as well as published material, and of the reference section of Cupar Library. I owe many thanks to Christopher Smout, Colin and Paula Martin, and Moray Stewart, especially for support and advice at early stages in the work; to Bill Baird for help with North Berwick material; to Alan Provan for photographs and other material from a variety of sources and detailed information on navigational lights; and to Ron Morris for information and advice on sources about events in World Wars I and II. Members of the Elie Historical Society have been very supportive and helpful. Jim Bell, the Chairman of the Society, has provided me with valuable material and very useful guidance on sources and other matters. Tom Maccabe's personal knowledge of the history of the later years has been invaluable and has kept me right on many points.

My very special thanks are due to David Thomson, who has a fund of knowledge on my subject and on sources, and has given me much help and advice, as well as unlimited access to his personal archive of documents, plans, and maps relating to Elie and Earlsferry, covering many centuries, and to his extensive collection of books; to Jimmy Linton for giving me much information not earlier recorded, as well as many photographs and allowing me to use his personal history as a fisherman to illustrate the decline of fishing in the area in the 20th century; and above all to Rosemary Black, who has spent many hours reducing my untidy manuscript to impeccable typescript, made many constructive suggestions about the presentation of my material, and arranged for its printing on behalf of the Society.

Finally, I express my warm thanks for the exemplary patience of my wife Kathleen, who has had a lot to put up with.

Archie Rennie

List of Illustrations

The numerals in parenthesis in the text refer to the figure numbers of the illustrations.
Cover illustration: the harbour in 1848 from an oil painting by Charles Blyth

Figure

1. Aerial view of Elie Bay in the 1980s

2. The harbour in the 1920s

Introduction

Elie Harbour lies on the northern coast of the Firth of Forth, about eleven and a half miles roughly south-west of Fife Ness, the most easterly point of the Fife peninsula. It is at a point where promontories on both shores narrow the Firth from its 15-mile wide entrance to a width of about nine miles, as shown in the sketch map (34) at the end of the book.

If you stand near the remains of the chapel on Chapel Ness surveying Elie Bay you see a long sandy beach in front of the town, a conspicuous feature of the aerial view in the illustration (1), taken about 1990. Chapel Ness is the rocky point near the top left-hand corner of the picture. At low tide you can see that the sands stretch right to the harbour which is about two-thirds of a mile away. The beach looks as if it had been designed by nature, except for the stone-built pier projecting towards you and the quay in front of the two buildings to the left of the pier. At any time before 1600 standing at the same point at high tide you would have seen a different view, with high water lapping the shore and stretching almost a mile and a half, all the way to the more distant headland of Elie Ness (not shown in the illustration), on which the lighthouse now stands. The low grassy mound now seen between the two conspicuous buildings before you at the harbour would have appeared as the highest point of a small rocky islet. As the tide receded you would have seen a bank known as the "*swarf*" emerge, connecting the islet to the shore, where today you see a sandy beach backed by a large grass-grown dune.

Elie Bay's value as a haven for shipping arises from the shelter provided by its enclosing headlands and the islet. That shelter became of real importance as a harbour only when there was traffic to take advantage of it. The first substantial traffic to use it that we know of with certainty was the pilgrim traffic from the south to the great shrine at St. Andrews. For most of the centuries the pilgrimages lasted the pilgrim boats came to land in the western corner of the bay at Earlsferry, just below the Chapel Ness viewpoint, where the remains of the pier they used can still (just) be seen.

The first strictly contemporary record that shows St. Andrews as an important place of pilgrimage is to be found in an Irish monastic chronicle which records the death of an Irish prince there in 967. The legend of St. Regulus and his near-miraculous voyage of 307 with some relics of St. Andrew from Patras in Greece to St. Andrews has to be a pious fable. The cult of St. Andrew in Scotland is now widely believed to have been inaugurated when Bishop Acca of Hexham fled from the Northumbrian king to Pictland in the reign of Angus I (730-61), bringing with him relics of St. Andrew which had been venerated at Hexham. This raises the interesting possibility that early users of the Earlsferry crossing before the end of the 8th century may well have included Northumbrians on pilgrimage to St. Andrews instead of Hexham, for whom a ferry across the Forth from North Berwick would have been very useful.

Pilgrimage to St. Andrews came to an abrupt end with the destruction of the shrine and relics in St. Andrews Cathedral in June 1559, one of the defining events of the Reformation in Scotland. This removed at a stroke much the greater part of the ferry's traffic, which in time led to its demise as a regular service.

The harbour we see today at the other end of the town, (2) was at first simply a natural harbour which used the shelter of the islet and the swarf. Its present shape has its origins in an ambitious scheme of development carried out by the barons of Ardross, the estate which included the Elie area, between about 1587 and 1600. Its present structure is the result of work carried out by William Baird, the owner of Elie and other extensive estates in the area, in the late 1850s.

1
The harbours and their early use

GENERAL DESCRIPTION

The natural harbour formed by Elie Bay on the south-eastern coast of Fife stretches between Elie Ness on the east and Chapel Ness on the west. It includes four practicable landing places which have been in use over the centuries as well as sandy beaches on which boats can readily land in suitable conditions. Towards the eastern end of the bay the former tidal islet of Elie Law, now connected to the shore by a substantial causeway, is a prominent feature. The islet and its "swarf", the natural rock ridge and sandbank which, even before the causeway was built, formed a passable dry route to the shore except at the higher tides, add greatly to the shelter provided by the two headlands. There are rocks and reefs in the western part of the bay which even small vessels have to treat with care. The most prominent of these is the East Vows, almost always above the surface of the sea and marked by a 19th century beacon which is also a tower of refuge for the shipwrecked. From the Vows a reef extends to the east where it ends in the Thill Rock marked by a large lighted buoy. Between the Thill Rock and the Apple Rock behind the pier extending from Elie Law there is a wide open passage giving easy access from the Firth to the present-day harbour, when the tide serves. The harbour dries out at low tide, although at neaps there is usually enough water close to the pier to float small craft.

In prehistoric times and indeed until much later in the harbour's history the normal landing place for the small craft then used would simply be the most convenient and sheltered part of the harbour's beaches, according to the conditions of wind and sea at the time. From the later centuries three structures can be identified, only one of which is now in use.

On the west, beside Chapel Ness, where the name of Boat Wynd commemorates the historic use of the inlet, lies a sheltered sandy landing place between the rocks with a narrow tidal passage to the open waters of the estuary. This passage provides a fairly deep channel which would allow medieval vessels access to the pier for much of the tidal cycle. The inlet served the medieval ferry to North Berwick from which Earlsferry takes its name, as well as local fishing boats, which would also serve as ferries at need. Until recently, the remains of a solidly built low stone pier, sloping with the shore, were clearly to be seen at the eastern side of the inlet, as is shown in the photograph (3) of an early 20th century fishing yawl - KY64 -moored alongside the ruins. These remains included a distinct alignment of large stone edging blocks (some displaced) and a single surviving stone pawl or bollard. The line can still be faintly traced, but most of the stones have been removed. The inlet was still in use by fishermen in the 20th century. This pier is shown in Roy's map of about 1750.

Further east towards the middle of the bay, not far from Earlsferry Town Hall, lie the Cockstail Rocks (4). Here the reefs enclosing a narrow creek have been cut back, notably on the east side where a rough quay has been formed in which iron mooring rings are still to be seen. This was a second harbour for Earlsferry at a later period. Though the street reaching the shore beside this little harbour is called Ferry Road this has no significance, the name being of recent origin. The former name was German Wynd, which was changed following the outbreak of the First World War. Sand has filled in the upper part of this harbour. It is reported that it was used at one time by coastal craft carrying coal from the Earlsferry mines, probably to other harbours on the Forth and Tay.

The main harbour (2) has a wide and easy entrance, very valuable for vessels seeking refuge, between the Thill Rock, marked by a red can buoy, and the pier. The Rock dries to 2 feet at the lowest tides, and a reef runs from it to the East Vows.

The modern harbour of Elie is first mentioned in the late 16th century, when the Elie Law site began to be developed, providing a harbour well suited for the larger ships of that time. Subsequent developments in the mid-19th century included a wide pier, a quay and parallel seawalls protecting a causeway. These enabled Elie Law to be connected to the shore by a metalled road and produced the substantial harbour we see today. Only one of the high seawalls is now visible, the one on the east side. On the west side, the seawall has been completely buried under the large sand dune that has accumulated over the 150 years since the causeway was built. The same accumulation of sand has reduced the accessible length of the 19th century quay by half and has made it necessary to dredge the harbour at intervals to keep a useful depth of water.

The fourth landing place, repeatedly identified by engineers as capable of providing a better and deeper harbour than any other in the East Neuk, is Wood Haven (also sometimes referred to as Wade's Haven) lying between Elie Law and Elie Ness. It has never been developed; but the rocky inlet on the west side behind the sailing clubhouse, known as Lucky's Hole, was used in earlier times for launching fishing boats and drawing them up for the winter. More recently, a concrete slip has been formed to make use of this advantageous site for launching small boats under certain conditions of wind and tide. The Ordnance Survey officers recording place names were told in 1853 that the name Wood Haven - earlier recorded in John Ainslie's map of Fife and Kinross published in 1775 - came from its use by timber-carrying ships, which could unload into the waters of this little bay when conditions were unsuitable for entering the main harbour. Boats would then tow or the tide would carry the timber to the shore.

EARLY USE

Though the earliest written record of the use of these harbours dates only from 1177, there can be no doubt that the bay would have been used by the early peoples of the area. The earliest settlers lived much by the shore. Shellfish, easily harvested, formed an important part of their diet. Archaeologists have identified what may be the remains of several shell middens in the harbour area. Finds from Fife and elsewhere in Scotland, like fishing weights and remains of boats, show that some of the early peoples knew how to make use of the resources of the sea. Their maritime capabilities are also shown even more clearly by

the way that early settlements were formed on the outlying islands of the Scottish coast.

In history, the earliest mention of any kind of settlement on Elie Bay relates to the Earlsferry area; and it seems reasonable to deduce that this was the most favoured site on the bay, and likely to be the area of the earliest settlements. Chapel Ness, though of no great height, shelters the western corner of the bay from the prevailing south-westerlies. A further consideration favouring this site is that access to fresh water is essential for any settlement; and the nearby spring-line stretching west from the 18th fairway of the golf course would probably be the nearest source of water that was easy to exploit. Further east shallow wells would be needed.

The earliest historical records that offer even a faint clue to the early use of Elie Bay as a harbour are in the histories of the later Roman Empire written by Ammianus Marcellinus in the second half of the fourth century, when the long Roman occupation of Southern Britain was nearing its end; but there is good reason to think that Elie Bay would have been familiar to some Roman shipmen about 200 years earlier than that. We know that Fife had a sizeable population in Roman times. At different periods the Romans established, or attempted to establish, a line of frontier control north of Perth. At one of these periods, possibly around 210 when the huge Roman fortress and supply depot at Carpow on the Tay near Newburgh was being built, the Roman commander found it necessary to send a sizeable force into East Fife. This is shown by the remains of the marching camp of that period at Edenwood near Cupar. His objective would have been to over-awe the local Picts and to deter interference with the Roman supply ships rounding Fife Ness on their way to Carpow. These ships would on occasion have to put in to the Fife shore near Fife Ness, and it is not fanciful to suppose that Roman warships and coasting supply ships would shelter at Elie from time to time. The supplies they carried would undoubtedly have included wine; and archaeological evidence for this traffic was discovered about a century ago in Constantine's Cave near Fife Ness. In it were found Roman amphora shards of the 2nd century AD, representing the remains of at least 6 large wine-containers, strongly suggesting a nearby shipwreck.

Towards the end of the centuries of Roman occupation, when the line of control was Hadrian's Wall, there were repeated raids on southern Britain from the north, from across the Irish Sea and from across the North Sea. Ammianus Marcellinus recorded that after the large-scale raids of 368, in which the occupying Romans suffered heavy losses, Pictish bands were roving at large through Roman Britain. They were rounded up by the re-organised and re-inforced Roman forces under the brilliant soldier Theodosius, who later became Roman Emperor.

T. C. Lethbridge, one of the academic historians who have written about the Picts, is confident that their raiding parties would have travelled by sea in substantial numbers of smallish boats of the curragh type, light wooden frameworks covered by skins. Bower records their use by the Picts and the Scots in 211 to cross the Tyne and by-pass Hadrian's Wall on their way to besiege York. Lethbridge's conclusions make good sense. It is clear that travelling by sea would cover the distances more easily and quickly and also enable the Pictish raiders to by-pass many miles of hostile territory south of the Forth before reaching the rich pickings of what is now Yorkshire and the lands further south. We can envisage flotillas of Pictish curraghs assembled in the Tay estuary and in Elie Bay and other natural harbours of east Fife - their best jumping off points in Pictish territory - before sailing to launch their raids well south of Hadrian's Wall.

From the Roman period onwards there can be little doubt that Elie Bay's natural advantages would bring to it plenty of Pictish maritime activity, both in fishing and in maintaining trading and other contacts across and up and down the Forth. There was a long period from about 600 until about 950 when the Picts of Fife (later in that period under the rule of Scottish kings of the MacAlpine dynasty) faced the powerful Anglian kingdoms of Bernicia and Northumbria which held the Lothian shore and its hinterland. During that period traffic across the estuary would be guarded and limited for much of the time. For a relatively short part of that period from about 658 to 685, when the southern part of the Pictish kingdom was under Northumbrian rule, there would be a good deal of Northumbrian traffic using the crossing; but the crushing victory of the Picts at Nechtansmere, traditionally believed to have been near Forfar, in 685 put an end to that.

The only Northumbrians left in Fife for the next few decades would be slaves. After that, apart from a single known instance of open warfare, the Northumbrians seem to have lived fairly peacefully with their northern neighbours. There is plenty to show sustained contacts between the two peoples, for example in the Northumbrian influence evident in Pictish carved stones, the most celebrated artefacts they left.

THE ORIGINS OF THE EARL'S FERRY

From the second half of the tenth century, when Kenneth II (971-995) established a peaceful Scottish claim to Lothian after Northumbria had ceased to be an independent kingdom, the crossing between Earlsferry and North Berwick would have become increasingly important. There had no doubt been pilgrim traffic bound for St. Andrews before that period, but from then on the number of pilgrims was to increase greatly. The last obstacles to peace in the area were removed in 1018 when Malcolm II, Malcolm Canmore's great-grandfather, defeated a Northumbrian army at Carham and established the border on the Tweed.

It was not long after the momentous victory at Carham, after Malcolm II's grandson King Duncan had been killed and succeeded by Macbeth (who had an equally good claim to the throne), that history contains the first record of what is still the most famous episode in the life of the ferry. It is in a chronicle composed in the 1360s by John de Fordun, supposed to have been a chaplain of St. Machar's Cathedral in Aberdeen, that we have the first written reference to the legendary escape across the estuary by Macduff, the Thane of Fife. Fordun's account says that Macbeth rightly suspected Macduff of seeking to put Malcolm Canmore on the throne. In Shakespeare's version, derived from Holinshed, Macduff had fled to his castle of Kennoway, and thence to Earlsferry. (Wood, the learned 19th century historian of the East Neuk, and Wilkie, writing in the 20th century, assert with some assurance that Macduff must have fled to his main castle of Rires, near Balcarres, much nearer the ferry. This seems much more likely.) Whatever the truth on this point, Macduff's cave in the cliffs of Kincraig is still pointed out as the place where he hid before he was ferried across the Forth by the boatmen of Earlsferry - not then known by that name - and so to Malcolm Canmore in England. This crossing would have been made in the early 1050s, prior to Malcolm's successful campaign in 1057.

GROWTH OF THE FERRY

How the ferry was organised in earlier centuries is not known. It was almost a century after Macduff's crossing that Duncan, Earl of Fife, who died in 1154, established two hospitals (hostels) intended for poor people and pilgrims using the crossing, one at North Berwick and one at Chapel Ness. Duncan had extensive estates in East Lothian, and a reliable ferry would be important to him. The need for the hospitals is a clear indication that pilgrims had been major users of the ferry for some time, on their way to the Shrine of St. Andrew. The earliest custodians of that shrine had been the Culdees, a post-Columban order of ecclesiastics found only in Ireland and Scotland, who prospered for two or three centuries around the year 1000. Some of their monastic establishments, all of which were independent, had considerable wealth and exercised great influence. They had several major establishments in Fife, including one at Balchrystie which is only 2½ miles from the ferry landing. By the time Earl Duncan endowed his hospitals, Culdee influence had greatly diminished; but it seems highly probable that at least up to the later decades of the 11th century the Culdees of Balchrystie would have played a part in providing food and lodging for pilgrims on the way to the shrine controlled by the Culdees at St. Andrews. The pilgrims' need for such services did not change over the centuries and it was an important duty of the religious to help pilgrims on their way. At St. Andrews itself the Culdees had a hostel for poor pilgrims.

It does appear that pilgrimage from distant areas to St. Andrews was well established long before Lothian became a recognised part of Scotland. It was commonplace for pilgrims to cross national borders freely; and the crossing from North Berwick to Earlsferry was an obvious route from many of the areas from which pilgrims came. In the medieval period and for several centuries, the ferrymen and their passengers and the local fishermen, whose boats must often have served the ferry, must have been the principal users of

the haven provided by Elie Bay. They would probably land on the beach as often as in the inlet beside Chapel Ness, according to tide and weather conditions. On the southern side Gullane Ness and the Dirleton Sands sheltered by the islet of Fidra were used as landing places before the landing was established at North Berwick.

In addition to pilgrims, ferry passengers in the medieval period would include parties involved in warfare, persons travelling on the king's judicial and other business, the Earls of Fife and their agents and others with scattered estates to look after and rents to collect, members of St. Baldred's Convent in North Berwick and other religious orders, other church dignitaries on diocesan business (often with revenues to collect) and traders. We should not underestimate the scale of medieval pilgrim traffic or the revenues it generated. One estimate reported by a historian of North Berwick suggests that there might have been as many as 10,000 pilgrims a year making the crossing, which would mean perhaps 100 a day or more at peak periods. In "Pilgrimage in Medieval Scotland" Peter Yeoman notes that "*A complex patchwork of ferries, roads, bridges, chapels, hospitals and inns was created and maintained to ease the way for the pilgrims to the national shrine*". All these installations and services had to be paid for, sometimes from charitable endowments; but many pilgrims had the means to pay. They were tourists with a purpose.

The most famous of the pilgrim ferries across the Forth was the Queen's Ferry, established by Queen Margaret, who died in 1093, to be a free crossing for pilgrims to St. Andrews from mid-southern and south-western Scotland and beyond. No doubt that narrow crossing had been in regular use long before that, particularly for members of the royal court at Dunfermline and other traffic crossing into Lothian and the south. Queen Margaret's son, King David I, put his mother's gift on a new basis when, in about 1130, he granted to the Abbot and Convent of Dunfermline "*the Passage and ship of Enderkeithing*", on condition that all travellers to and from the court should have free passage over the water.

Earl Duncan's foundation of his two hospitals, before 1154, seems to have followed Queen Margaret's or King David's example. Certainly the later proceedings of his son, also Earl Duncan, seem to have been modelled on the actions of King

David four decades earlier. This is not surprising. The Earls of Fife were close to the Scottish kings in many ways. It is noteworthy that in 1152, on the death of his eldest son Prince Henry, King David "*took forthwith his son's first-born, Malcolm, and giving him as guardian, Duncan, Earl* (of Fife) *with a numerous army, commanded that this boy should be conducted round the provinces of Scotland, and proclaimed to be the heir to the kingdom.*"

In 1177 the second Earl Duncan granted the hospitals and the "*hospital lands of Ardross*" to St. Baldreds Convent, the nunnery in North Berwick, and described them as founded by his father for the reception of paupers and pilgrims. The Convent is almost invariably so-called, although on its seal and in all formal documents, it is designated "*the monastery*". It appears to have been founded by the first Earl Duncan. Both the initial foundation and Earl Duncan's subsequent grant took place during the reign of King David I, when Culdee establishments all over Scotland were being suppressed in favour of the newer monastic orders favoured by Queen Margaret and her descendants. Balchrystie was one of the properties transferred from the Culdees of Lochleven to the Augustinian Priory of St. Andrews at this time. In Wood's "History of the East Neuk of Fife", he suggests that the Culdees of Balchrystie might have been down-graded into the keepers of the pilgrim hospital. This would have been a means of providing for their future subsistence, but a great loss of status. The endowments granted to the Convent at this time and later by Earl Duncan's successors included extensive lands and church revenues from East Lothian and Eastern Fife, much greater than would be needed simply to support the hospitals. The sources do not reveal whether any share in the right to operate the ferry was also granted to the Convent. There is later evidence that half at least of the right to operate the ferry was retained by the Earl of Fife. The name Earlsferry itself does suggest that the ferry was the Earl's property.

One special group of travellers for whom the Earl's ferry would be of particular value were the officials of the cathedral, diocese and priory of St. Andrews, where Scotland's senior bishop, and later the archbishop, had his seat. A very large and productive area south of the Forth was included in the diocese. Its extent was clearly defined when Charles I split the diocese - at that period a diocese of the established Episcopal Church of Scotland - in 1639, and made the areas south of the Forth into the new diocese of Edinburgh. These areas were described as "*the Sheriffdoms of Edinburgh, Linlithgow, Stirling, and Berwick, the constabulary of Haddington, and Baillerie of Lauderdale*". Before the reformation the St. Andrews bishops, cathedral and priory received much of their considerable revenues from this wealthy part of Scotland and had very valuable rights of patronage there. The Provost of the cathedral had charge of its finances, and he and his agents would find the ferry a quick and convenient way to reach much of the southern part of the diocese.

THE PLACE NAMES

In 1228, a charter by Malcolm, Earl of Fife, confirming Earl Duncan's grant of 1177, calls the land at Chapel Ness "*the hospital land of Ardross*". Ardross was the name of the large estate granted by Malcolm Canmore to Merleswein, a Northumbrian who accompanied the English Princess Margaret to Scotland before she became Malcolm's Queen. The ruins of Ardross Castle are still to be seen about 1½ miles east of the lighthouse. The language of the charter suggests that the place name Earlsferry had not yet come into use by this date. In 1250 Earlsferry is mentioned, in the Latin, as "*passagium comitis*"; and in 1295 there is mention of "*the muir of the hospital of Earlsferry*". There is a curious later indication that the "*hospital land of Ardross*" included (with a good deal more) the area west of the chapel ruins now known as the Dome Park, enclosed by the high curving stonewall with the pair of substantial gate posts. In 1786 the Earl of Balcarres, crippled by debts largely incurred by supporting the cause of the exiled Stuarts, had to sell his estates to his brother Robert Lindsay, who had made a fortune in India. Concerned to retain a foothold in his native area, the Earl purchased the enclosed land at Chapel Ness. He subsequently had it listed rather ambitiously as his seat in Scotland, under the name "*Earlsferry Abbey*". There was of course no building of that name; but this seems to be a reference back to the hospital owned by the Convent of St. Baldred.

The name Elie has older origins, connected with the harbour area. Two of the more plausible theories about the name take us back to the time when the Pictish tongue had been displaced in Fife by Gaelic.

This must have been a gradual process, but before the end of the tenth century, Gaelic had become the language of the ruling classes at least. One theory is that the name derives straightforwardly from the Gaelic "*eilean*", an island or islet, and simply refers to Elie Law, the tidal islet that is such a conspicuous identifying feature of the bay. Another suggests the name is possibly derived from "*ealadh*", meaning a place where corpses, usually of people of distinction, were landed on the way to burial at a particular shrine, in this case the great pilgrimage shrine of St. Andrews. Later the name in English became Ely or Elie, meaning (in English) an island. It seems highly probable that at some point the Gaelic word, whatever it was, simply slipped into the English form, as Gaelic gradually fell into disuse. That the Gaelic form was "*eilean*" is in some measure supported by the long-standing usage of the expression "the Elie of Ardross", meaning the tidal islet, but later used to refer to the burgh.

MEDIEVAL FERRY RULES AND CHARGES
In his verse history of Scotland, written around 1400, Andrew Wyntoun, Prior of the Monastery of St. Serf on its island in Loch Leven, gives this account of the Earl's Ferry.

> "*That passage syne was comownly*
> *In Scotland called the Erlys-Ferry*
> *Off that ferry for to knawe*
> *Baith the statute and the lawe,*
> *A bate suld be on ilke side*
> *For to wait and tak the tyde,*
> *Til mak' them fracht that would be*
> *Fra land to land beyhond that se*
> *Fra that the sowth bate ware sene*
> *The landys undyre sayle betwene*
> *Fra the sowth as than passand*
> *Toward the north the trade haldand,*
> *The north bate suld be redy made*
> *Towart the sowth to hald the trade*
> *And thare suld nane pay mare*
> *Than foure pennies for thare fare,*
> *Quha evyr for his frawcht wald be*
> *For caus frawchtyd owre that se.*"

Wyntoun was not a great poet; but as Prior of St. Serf's he was well placed to know all about the Earl's Ferry. The rule that the boat from the north should set off when the boat from the south was sighted was clearly intended to ensure that there would not be too much delay before a boat was available on either side. This indicates both that there were considerable numbers of passengers by 1400 and that the ferry had dedicated boats and was in regular use. It is interesting that a century and a half later, when Parliament decided in 1551 to fix the rates for the Tay crossing at Broughty Ferry it decreed "*For ilk man and horse, eight pennies, and for ilk man and woman be themselves, four pennies*".

In the year 1426 the Parliament of King James I enacted that "*all Boatemen and Ferryares quhair Horse are ferried sall have for ilk boate a treene brigge* (i.e. a wooden gangplank) *quhair with they maie receive within thair Boates travellers Horse through the realme, unhurt and unskaithed, under the peine of xl.s of ilk Boate*". The default penalty of 40 shillings was pretty steep, considering that the ferry fare for a man and a horse was only 8 pence. It is not difficult to deduce that the main beneficiaries of the law were the nobles, gentry and other people of wealth. A similar law passed under King James III in 1467 makes this explicit. It was enacted expressly "*for the utilite and profit of the Kingis Hieness and his lieges, quhilkis divers tymis passis over the feryis with their horss*".

SANCTUARY
The passage from Wyntoun is quoted by Chapman in his account of Elie and East of Fife, published in 1892. Chapman also has some account of the privilege of sanctuary, which he says was granted to the burgh; but the long established tradition is that the right originated in a grant by Malcolm Canmore to his loyal supporter Macduff, and was intended for the benefit of Macduff's kin. It is often later described as part of the law of Clan Macduff, whose medieval chief was the Earl of Fife, and to allow a fugitive from justice to cross halfway over the Forth before a boat might lawfully set out in pursuit. There seems no doubt that it really did exist, for it is recorded by George Buchanan, the most reliable of the early Scottish historians (despite his partiality against Mary Queen of Scots). Detailed accounts of this right of sanctuary being claimed are recorded for 1391, 1421, and, Chapman says, 1728, which was of course long after the Convent had disappeared from the scene.

2
The fourteenth and fifteenth centuries

THE WAR OF INDEPENDENCE

In the later Middle Ages there are interesting records of the use of the Earlsferry passage at a time of great troubles for Scotland. For a number of years in the period after the death of Alexander III at Kinghorn in 1286, Edward I of England was *de facto* sovereign of Scotland, and acknowledged as such, under compelling constraints, by large numbers of the nobility and other landowners. In his capacity as sovereign Edward held the Earl of Fife's castle of Rires on behalf of Duncan, a minor, heir to the earldom but not yet *infeft* in his lands and titles. Edward dated charters from Rires, which would be a convenient headquarters for some of his operations, because of its ease of communications with the south by way of the ferry. However, it was in 1302 while he was at Dunfermline, the seat of the Scottish kings at this period, that we have a record of a ferry crossing on his business. On 20th November of that year, in the account books of the Prince of Wales, later Edward II, the record shows "*For the passage of John Dengaigne, the Prince's valet de chambre, and his grooms, bringing £400 for the household from London across the Forth at Earl's Ferry, 6s.8d* ". 6s. 8d. would pay for ten horsemen and their mounts. It should be noted that at this date English coins and Scottish coins had the same value. It had long been the Scottish kings' policy to keep their currency at parity with that of England. It was after long years of decline and debasement that in 1603 the rate was fixed at 12 pounds Scots to 1 pound sterling.

Again in March 1303 4, Alexander de Convers engaged two vessels to carry 2000 merks (£1333) from North Berwick to Passagium Comitis (Earlsferry) for the use of Edward I at St. Andrews. This, incidentally, shows that by this date the name of Earlsferry had become established as the name of the northern ferry terminal rather than the name of the crossing itself.

At the time when Edward I was in Fife, and particularly when he was campaigning further north, the Earlsferry passage would be of some importance to him. Military and administrative travellers between Scotland north of the Tay and Edward's capital in London, and the resources he drew upon in England, could get quickly up the east coast of Scotland by a route easily traced today. From the landing at Earlsferry, the Cadger's Road led to the Earl of Fife's castle at Rires and thence by Largoward, Peat Inn and Strathkinness to the tidal ford or coble ferry across the Eden Estuary at the Coble Shore, and so by Earlshall and Tentsmuir to Ferry-Port-on-Craig (Tayport) and the crossing to Broughty Ferry. Royal messengers with horses at command could probably cross from Angus to North Berwick in the course of a summer's day.

Events in Fife do not figure greatly in the War of Independence, which began during Edward I's occupation. Though the main objectives of the Scots had been achieved by the Battle of Bannockburn in 1314, the long dispute with England was not formally ended until 1328. Throughout that troubled period and the decades of intermittent struggles with the English monarchs that continued into the 16th century the ferry passage would no doubt be very busy from time to time with fugitives and military travellers; and the streams of pilgrims continued. As late as 1336, when Edward III of England controlled most of Scotland south of the Forth, the Sheriff of Edinburgh accounted to him for one-half of the profits of "*the ferry of North Berwick*". This seems to indicate that at that date at least half of the ferry rights were owned by the earl, who was in arms against Edward. The English king was attempting to take over Scotland as his grandfather had done, and had declared the earl's property forfeit to the crown. Here we also have an indication that the profits of the ferry were worth having.

EARLSFERRY BURGH – THE ROLE OF CRAIL

Burgh life was steadily developing in Scotland during this troubled time; but Earlsferry does not appear in a (possibly incomplete) list of burghs found in documents of 1357. It is unclear whether it had obtained burghal status by this date. The hospitals were still provided by the Convent of North Berwick. There is a Parliamentary reference to Earlsferry as a burgh, with a procurator, in 1541.

In the Middle Ages, Crail played an important part in the harbour affairs of Earlsferry and later of Elie. It was already a place of importance before the reign of King David I (1124 -1153), because its royal castle was the centre of extensive estates, with the king's barns, the king's mills, and the king's warren. David I frequently stayed there. It was important as a fishing harbour, and for fish exports; Crail and the Isle of May were resorted to for the fishing, particularly of herring, by boats from France and Holland as well as Scotland and England.

Crail was the seat of a royal constabulary extending as far as Kincraig Point. When it became a royal burgh under a charter granted by Robert the Bruce in 1310 it was formally granted trading jurisdiction, which the constabulary had probably already exercised, over the area extending from the Putikin Burn (which appears to be the Kenly Burn near Boarhills) to the River Leven. It appears unlikely that these rights would affect the ferry, because their primary purpose was to ensure that shipping engaged in overseas trade paid customs duty on exports at the royal burgh, which collected the customs on behalf of the king. Until an Act of Parliament in 1597, there was no customs duty on imported goods. These rights were still being claimed by Crail in the 16th century, but those over Earlsferry were then being disputed, until finally extinguished by the burgh's royal charter of 1589. The last rights over Elie were finally commuted by agreement in 1607. Crail's general rights over the area and harbours "both new and old" between Leven and Boarhills were re-stated with some reservations in a Royal Charter of 1685 granted to the burgh by King Charles II; but the reservations seem to have prevented Crail from exercising any rights in face of the charters of Elie and Earlsferry.

Crail was an important trading harbour, and among the East Fife ports it pioneered the trade to England and the nearer parts of Europe that would later become important for Earlsferry and Elie. Some indication of the goods that were exported is to be found in an ordinance passed in 1380 by the city of Rheims, which regulated the sale of salmon, herring and cod imported from Scotland, and also of wool, leather and hides. In Scotland the "*great customs*" or export dues collected for the king from the trade of Scottish ports were paid upon wool, wool-fells, skins and hides. Imports included commodities such as iron and salt, luxuries including wines and rich cloths, and other specialist manufactures like haberdashery, and arms and armour.

Custom accounts of the Fife ports of around 1400 show that Inverkeithing, Kinghorn, St. Andrews and Cupar, with its harbour at Guardbridge, shared overseas trade in exports of dutiable goods at £334, compared with £1168 for Edinburgh, £660 for Dundee and £448 for Perth. Probably because the East Neuk exports were mainly of non-dutiable goods no East Neuk port is listed. By 1498 the ports were probably a good deal more active. In that year, despite the outbreak of war with England, Englishmen coming with merchandise in their ships or boats to the ports or havens of Pittenweem, Anstruther, Earlsferry and Crail were given protection in the form of safe conducts or passports, during a period of truce. This reference to Earlsferry suggests that at the beginning of the 16th century the harbour of Elie had not yet been developed, although a reference to the "port and haven of the Elye" appears as early as 1491. No doubt, given the restricted entrance to the pier beside Chapel Ness, ships intending to land goods in Elie Bay would sometimes choose to take advantage of the open entrance to the shelter provided by Elie Law and the swarf connecting the Law to the shore. By this period ships trading to England and the continent had become quite sizeable, and their masters would be chary of venturing among the reefs of Earlsferry except under favourable conditions.

3

The sixteenth century – Elie on the rise

THE DISHINGTON BARONS

The disastrous battles of Flodden in 1513 and Pinkie in 1547 must have badly affected the progress of trade and development generally in Fife, in common with most of Scotland. The loss of so many members of the landed families, the ransoms for prisoners, and so much expensive military equipment, horses and other property lost or destroyed, straddling two generations, inevitably meant a slowdown in many desirable improvements. A mitigating factor was that the leaders in economic innovation were frequently to be found in religious foundations, less likely to be affected by the casualty lists. In the East Neuk, the Priory of the Isle of May (later to be of Pittenweem), with its lands on the mainland, was active in promoting fishing, coal-mining, and salt manufacture; and the North Berwick convent was active too. The landowners also became increasingly active in such developments; but the first half of the sixteenth century saw many interruptions to peace and progress.

The title of the Dishingtons of Ardross, proprietors of extensive lands, including Elie, came from their ancestor Sir William Dishington's charter of Ardross of 1368. His mother was a sister of Robert the Bruce, and he enjoyed valuable royal patronage. Along with several other East Neuk lairds a later William Dishington of Ardross fell at Pinkie in 1547. His grandson Thomas, who was a minor at the death of his father (also Thomas), could not take charge until 1582. He died before 1591 and was succeeded by his son Thomas, also a minor, who did not come of age until 1598.

THE BUILDING OF THE HARBOUR

It was the Thomas who took charge of his estate in 1582 who took the first steps towards the development of Elie Harbour. As soon as he was of capacity to act, Thomas petitioned the Convention of Royal Burghs, which had special responsibilities for overseas trade as well as the power to raise money from its constituent burghs, for help in "*the upbigging of the haven called Ely*". The Convention agreed to help, understanding "*the samyn to be ane very commodious harbery, gif the samyn were upbiggit, for all schippis and boittis saifty in stormes of wether*". The language used, particularly the clause "*gif* (if) *the samyn* (same) *were upbiggit* (built up)" implies that there had been no building work before that date to improve the natural harbour. The estate papers in the Scottish Record Office contain no information about any assistance Thomas may have received from the Convention.

In *Archaeological Notes on some harbours in Eastern Scotland* Angus Graham records that Elie came on record as "*port and hevin*" in 1491, and suggests that Dishington began his building work in the year he submitted his petition to the Convention. It is perhaps more likely that preparations for the work and raising money would take some time before work could begin, but it probably began some time before 1587.

Thomas entered into an agreement about his port with the royal burgh of Crail. This provided that in the event of Dishington obtaining the erection of Elie (meaning erection by royal charter) into a free burgh, port and haven, Crail would surrender its rights over the port of Elie. There was an important proviso that no inhabitant of Crail should be charged with harbour dues in Elie, nor any inhabitant of Elie charged with dues in Crail, and that a yearly feu-duty of forty shillings should be paid by the proprietor of the port of Elie to the burgh of Crail. Thus Crail's superior status continued to be recognised. Thomas must have begun building work on the harbour structures not long after his agreement with Crail. There is evidence in a Royal Charter of 1598 that the harbour works, which included a pier, a quay, and a wall along the swarf (later known as "*the Swarf Dyke*"), had been far advanced by that year. In that year Thomas Dishington III was served heir to his father and sold part of Ardross, including the harbour, to his father-in-law.

William Scott – the Elie Royal Charters

In 1598 William Scott of Grangemuir (near Pittenweem), had paid Thomas 37,000 merks, about 25,000 pounds Scots or around 2000 pounds sterling, for the western part of Ardross called "*the Elie*". Scott was James VI's Director of Chancery. The royal charter Scott obtained at that date describes his purchase as including the "*villam de Elie, eius tenementa, domos et hortes, lie Elie Law et tutum lie swarf ei adjacent., molendinam de Elie*", etc. Thus Scott had acquired the town of Elie, with all its tenements (holdings), houses and gardens, Elie Law and the entire adjoining bank called the swarf, the mill of Elie, etc. The charter also lists "*omnes portus, stationes, et navalia*", which it translates into Scots as "*lie portis, hevynnis and harbareis*".

This charter was of fundamental importance to Elie. In addition to recording Scott's new property it granted his town of Elie the status and rights of a free baronial burgh with a free port "*cum libero portu nuncupandum Burgum et Portum de Elie*", i.e. to be known as the Burgh and Port of Elie, with all the rights pertaining to a free baronial burgh and port. Becoming a free baronial burgh conveyed certain privileges in trade, especially in inland goods and some bulky items of foreign trade. It was also important for Scott to obtain the status of a free port for his harbour, though this did not wholly extinguish the rights of Crail. Crail's supervisory jurisdiction was removed; but the separate obligation to pay Crail a feu-duty did not end until 1607, when it was remitted in perpetuity by the magistrates of Crail on account of the pains taken in Parliament by their friend Mr. William Scott. The reciprocal agreement about freedom from harbour dues for inhabitants of one burgh using the other burgh's harbour remained and has never been formally extinguished.

The charter's reference to the mill is not the first record of its existence. The first reference we have is in a document of 1584; but it may have been some time before then that it was established, beside the Loch Run, the man-made outlet of Kilconquhar Loch that drove it, close to the point where the Run still discharges into the harbour. The Run was an abundant source of fresh water, important for any ship taking its departure from Elie for a long voyage.

Scott was granted a second royal charter in 1601, which contained a reference to further building work needed at the harbour to bring the work "*to full perfection*", and also to the work already carried out by Scott to this end. This suggests that Thomas Dishington probably had not commanded the resources needed to complete his ambitious plans, and shows that it was his wealthy father-in-law who actually completed the earliest scheme of harbour development at Elie Law. However the charter of 1598 does show that by that date Thomas Dishington had "*upbiggit*" "*the harbery*" with substantial works, enough for the king to recognise it as a port. There is a further indication that Thomas was acknowledged to be the founder of the harbour in a late 17th century reference to Elie manse as "*lying above the Currie Heughs*" (i.e. the quarries working the hard reddish-brown stone of the foreshore below the Terrace) and close to the harbour "*biggit of auld*" by Thomas Dishington of Ardross.

The Structures of the Harbour

There is no contemporary description of the works carried out by Thomas and his father-in-law, but one of the documents provides clues. In James VI's charter of 1601 to "*our weelbelovit Maister William Scott of Elie*", Scott is given power to uplift a "*towst and dutie on all merchandise arriving in the port*". The dues levied were to be "*employed in building and upholding the haven, shore, and bulwark thereof....*". This reference indicates that there were three structures to be built and maintained, and later documentary evidence and maps confirm that Thomas's works included a pier (enclosing the haven), a quay (the shore) and the wall on the line of the swarf (the bulwark). There is a later mention, in a document of 1615 consolidating the Scott holdings of Elie and Ardross into a single barony of Ardross, with the burgh of barony called Elie, with "*harbour, pier, etc*".

A pier suitable for loading and unloading ships would not have been an essential element for an effective harbour, for these activities were provided for by the "*shore*"; but a protective pier to increase the shelter provided by the harbour was constructed on a reef projecting north from the Apple Rock (to be seen behind the granary), on the same line as, but shorter and much narrower than, the present pier constructed in the 1850s. This pier is shown in plans prepared in 1815 for the improvement of the harbour (5). It was about 160 feet long, and wide enough to be used for loading and unloading cargoes. The early quay - about 130 feet long - is now buried within the 1850s quay. An indication of where the edge of that earlier quay was is provided by one surviving stone pawl (bollard) to be seen beside the car parking area of the granary flats. The pawl would probably be only a few feet inside the edge of the quay. There is plenty of later documentary evidence for the existence of the swarf dyke, along which on the harbour side ran a cart road to the quay and pier. This track was in use until the causeway was built, though in its last years it was regularly flooded at high tides. In Dishington's time and for many years thereafter there was adjoining the landward end of the swarf a field of some size to the east, in an area now part of the foreshore, which stretched from the swarf to the "*mid rock*" in Wood Haven.

Ships of the period, like 19th and 20th century puffers, were accustomed to take the ground at low water, while loading and unloading either on to a quay or into carts drawn up alongside. Unloading into the carts alongside would be possible with the minimum of lift from the ship's derricks, and the easiest way to unload heavy goods like timber. Timber was less likely to go astray than more portable cargoes and could be unloaded with little supervision. Lighter and more valuable merchandise would probably be unloaded under supervision on to the quay. An example of the rig of the larger foreign-going ships of the time is shown in the illustration (6), from a tombstone carving.

Possibly from the beginning, but certainly in later years, a cart track over the sands and through the rocks of the foreshore to the foot of School Wynd was used for the heavy goods, particularly timber. The seaward continuation of School Wynd was known at various times as Auchmuty's Wynd, Well Wynd, and, significantly, Baltic Wynd. Timber from Norway or the Baltic formed a large part of the import trade of Elie for many years; and among the merchants' houses of South Street there was one that had a saw pit in its yard. As earlier noted, timber was sometimes also unloaded into the waters of Wood Haven, when conditions made it difficult to use the main harbour.

HARBOUR DUES

The power in the charter of 1601 to charge harbour dues was granted initially for a period of 19 years. The first dues listed in the charter are tonnage dues on all vessels entering at two shillings per ton of capacity, and on their cargoes at two shillings per ton. Vessels leaving paid two shillings per ton on their cargoes; and there were also dues of twelve pennies per ton, apparently for both incoming and outgoing traffic, relating to merchandise carried for "*freemen, unfreemen and strangers and sic like*". Merchandise means merchant goods ready for sale, and because of their higher value it seems they paid an additional duty on top of the regular duty applicable to all cargoes. Oddly, there seems to be no discrimination in favour of freemen of the burgh. There may not have been a sufficient number of freemen merchants in the burgh to support the trade it hoped to attract. The important trade in timber "*frae*" Norway and other parts paid dues at the rate of one piece of timber in every hundred, thus "*of ilk hundred geistis* (joists) *ane*", "*of ilk hundred daillis* (deals) *ane*", and "*of ilk hundred wainscottis* (panelling boards) *ane* ". There were also dues of 16 pennies per chalder of victual sold within the port. (A chalder varied in capacity from place to place and from commodity to commodity. In Fife a chalder of oatmeal equated roughly to one ton.) Eight pennies was charged for "*the skipper and marines*". The charter concludes with legal powers to William Scott to enforce these dues.

With the charter of 1601 the harbour of Elie was established on a firm legal footing with the essential financial powers to operate, as it has continued to do, although through many vicissitudes, to the present day.

3. Yawl at the Chapel Ness landing and Earlsferry House

4. Cockstail Rocks harbour with moored fishing boats

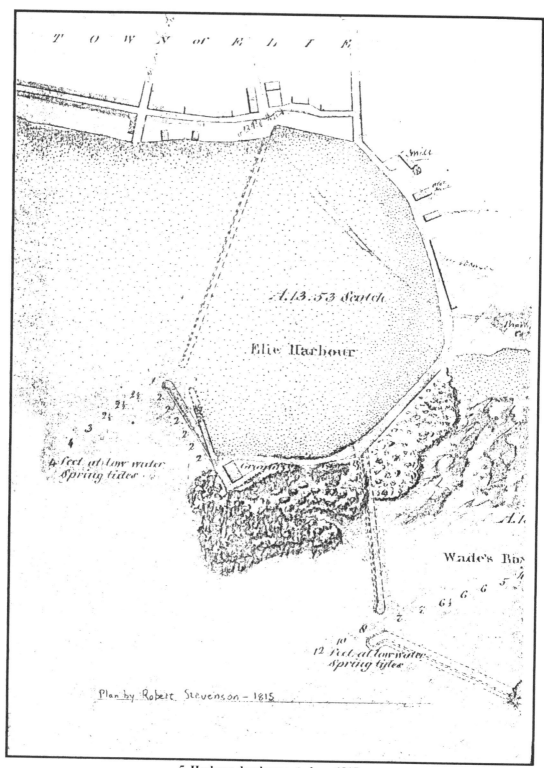

5. Harbour development plan - 1815

4

The sixteenth century – Earlsferry in decline

DECAY OF THE EARL'S FERRY

While the barons of Ardross were developing the harbour potential of Elie Law and the adjoining swarf, the Earl's ferry had fallen into decay. This was a direct consequence of the Scottish Reformation. The defining events of that Reformation took place in the period 1559-1561. The last Provincial Council of the ancient church took place in the spring of 1559. Its decrees were carefully framed but mostly ineffectual. The formal end of the Roman Church and the establishment of the new Protestant form of religion were decreed by the Three Estates in August 1560. It was to be more than a century before a final settlement was reached on several of the issues that remained in dispute; but one matter of great importance to Earlsferry had been settled beyond recall. In St. Andrews, on the 15th June 1559, the Protestant mob, in the words of one historian of the city, "*roused to fury, put an end to eight centuries of ecclesiastical history. They stripped the great cathedral of all its treasures, which they stole or burnt, leaving it an empty shell*". These events meant the end of pilgrimages to St. Andrews and led in time to the end of the Earl's Ferry. Pilgrimage was made illegal by a decree of 1581, which clearly implies that some centres had continued to attract pilgrims up to that date.

ALEXANDER WOOD'S CHARTER OF EARLSFERRY

Walter Wood tells the story of the events that followed. Interestingly, the 16th century document he quotes does not expressly relate the decline of the ferry to the ending of pilgrimages. Perhaps in 1572 it was taboo to suggest that the Reformation could have had any detrimental effects, though it would be very well known to everyone what the ending of pilgrimages had meant to Earlsferry.

" *In 1572 the laird of Grange, Alexander Wood, obtained a royal charter of Earlsferry, which* narrates that 'the Earl's ferry for many bygone years had been so rarely used, that the sailors and ferrymen had been forced to leave it, and to betake themselves to other places for a maintenance, whence not only had the commonweal of this kingdom, and the whole district of Fife, suffered loss, but also the town of the said ferry is reduced to nothing; and our faithful subjects can rarely be ferried across there when occasion demands. Wherefore, in order that opportunity may be given for bringing the ferry-men to the said ferry, and that passage may be had at all times; and that the harbour thereof may be rebuilt, and our lieges may resort thither in greater numbers, and be able to dwell there, so that by them foreign enemies may be the better hindered from landing and devastating the country, we have given to Mr. Alexander Wood', etc. In the same year Wood obtained a precept from the sheriff in his favour, on a claim to be infeft by the bailies of Earlsferry in the port and anchorage thereof, and in the sum of £10 Scots, payable yearly from the profits of the ferry to the commendator and convent of Culross, which duty they had made over to the said laird; and the following year there are letters of advocation at the instance of the provost, bailies, and community of Crail, and the bailies of Earlsferry, discharging the sheriff from proceeding further in that matter, on the ground that Crail had been created a free burgh, and that Earlsferry with the port thereof was part and pendicle of the same. This dispute would seem to have been in existence for a hundred years before this time, for there is extant an instrument of protest, taken before Parliament at Stirling in 1451, by the procurator for the burgh of Earlsferry, bearing that the Abbot of Culross, after summoning the said burgh to answers for the unjust detention of £10, had not appeared to support the summons.*"

These disputes were probably brought to an end by a royal charter granted in 1589 (the original records of the burgh having been accidentally burnt), in which the former privileges were confirmed, and Earlsferry erected into a free royal burgh and harbour; with the declaration that they had existed past the memory of men"

Alexander Wood, described as "*the laird of Grange*", was the second son of the famous Sir Andrew Wood of Largo, and had been the last pre-Reformation Vicar of North Berwick. This was essentially an ecclesiastical office of profit. The parish duties were carried out by a curate, named as Sir George Lyall ("*Sir*", was a title of respect for a minister of religion). Alexander Wood was also the Vicar of Largo. By December 1557 he was described as "*Vicar pensioner of North Berwick*". Among other transactions privatising church lands he bought the property of Grange, the Convent's farm and lands near Earlsferry, from the convent for £1,000 in 1560. The Convent needed the money to repair their properties in North Berwick; but by 1582 according to George Law "*the nunnery of North Berwick was in ruins; it is described as Funditus eversum*".

It is not easy to make sense of what Wood's "East Neuk" has to say about the transactions of Alexander Wood concerning the ferry and harbour of Earlsferry. Wood's reference to a protest in 1451 is a mistake, for 1541 was the date in question. The information that the "*commendator and convent of Culross*" had the right to receive a payment of £10 yearly from the profits of the ferry tells, firstly, that the ferry had been profitable, and secondly, that the right to operate the ferry had at some date transferred to the burgh, possibly through a transaction involving the Convent of Culross, subject to an annual payment of £10 by the burgh. The dissolution of monasteries, abbeys, and convents that followed the Reformation did not extinguish their property rights. It usually transferred them into lay ownership, commonly that of a local landowner, who held the property "*in commendam*" and was titled the "*commendator*". The words "*and convent*" show that the surviving members of the Culross convent shared the property rights with the commendator, an arrangement intended to provide for their subsistence and prevent hardship; but the property in due course, as the members of the Convent died out, would come into the outright ownership of the commendator. After the Reformation there were many such property transactions, usually to the benefit of

influential noblemen and other landowners. The commendator of Culross was Alexander Colville, who was apparently bought off by a payment of ten shillings a year to him and the Convent, with one penny to the king.

BURGHAL STATUS OF EARLSFERRY

These references, and the later references to actions raised by the burgh of Crail in 1573 and to an action raised in Parliament by the procurator of Earlsferry in 1541 confirm that Earlsferry was established as a burgh before the charter of 1589; but they give no help to the proposition that it was a royal burgh before then. Not all burghs were royal burghs. In addition to establishing their own royal burghs, the early kings from David I onwards gave leave to a number of abbeys, cathedrals, and great lay lords to have burghs of their own. In the 1589 charter by James VI it is recorded that '*the Burgh of Earlsferry had been erected of old into a free burgh, and had been so reputed beyond the memory of man*'. All of this says nothing about what kind of burgh Earlsferry was.

The fact that the royal burgh of Crail claimed rights over Earlsferry and more significantly that the bailies of Earlsferry joined with the bailies of Crail in an action in 1573 in which both parties declared that "*Earlsferry with the port thereof was part and pendicle of Crail*" makes clear that the status of Earlsferry as a recognised free burgh before that date had not been enough to supersede the established rights of the royal burgh of Crail. It could be interpreted to mean that Earlsferry claimed to share in Crail's rights, as part of the royal burgh. In the royal charters setting up baronial and ecclesiastical burghs there was always a clause "*securing the liberties of our burghs*", preserving the rights any royal burgh had in the new burgh's area. This seems an obvious foundation for the declaration of 1573. It seems possible that the powerful and wealthy Convent of St. Baldred might have obtained the right to establish a free burgh at the harbour of Earlsferry, as, for example, the Abbey of Lindores did at Newburgh in 1266, but the new burgh simply remained subordinate to Crail. Colin McWilliam, writing about the burgh architecture of Scotland, lists Earlsferry as one of the ecclesiastical burghs seized by James VI in 1589 and made into a royal burgh. (The list also includes St. Andrews.)

THE CONVENT AND FERRY TRAFFIC

It was only in 1588 that the Convent had finally ceased to exist, when James VI granted to Alexander Home, brother of the last Prioress and a royal favourite, the whole of the lands that remained the Convent's property. Since 1548 Alexander Home had been gathering in parts of the Convent's estates, by purchase under feu title but later by means which also included personal payments to the Prioress and to individual nuns. Home's royal grant was not quite the final stroke. In 1596 the former prioress and one surviving nun made over to the king himself the ecclesiastical revenues of the parishes of Logie, Largo and Kilconquhar, the very last remnants of the Convent's once large revenues. The burgh of Earlsferry's Royal Charter of 1589 seems to fit in well with this long process of dissolution and take-over.

With the Reformation and the destruction of the relics at St. Andrews the formerly large traffic of pilgrims had dried up. The collection of diocesan revenues for St. Andrews and other traffic on diocesan business must have been greatly reduced if not entirely suspended. The number of landowners, lay or ecclesiastical, who owned lands on both sides of the estuary had been reduced. Because of the usefulness of the most easterly short crossing of the Forth there would no doubt still be some passenger traffic; and the passage was also useful for some cargoes. In particular, it seems highly likely that coal workings near Earlsferry had begun to support coal exports across the Forth before, perhaps well before, the end of the 16th century.

COAL TRAFFIC

Among the industrial enterprises of the Convent of St. Baldred was the manufacture of floor and wall tiles, for which the Convent had four kilns. These kilns would require a good deal of fuel, as would the domestic life of the Convent, for heating, cooking, and the baking of bread. Since coal was won on lands at Earlsferry belonging to the Convent it seems very probable that, like the Priory at Pittenweem, the Convent would have its own coal mines on its own land; and it would be simple to ship coal across to North Berwick for its own use and, by natural extension, for sale to other users and for charitable giving to the poor. To carry coal across the Forth from Earlsferry makes good

sense, for the crossing to North Berwick is both shorter, and because of the prevailing winds easier for a sailing craft than the passage from and back to Cockenzie, the nearest coal port in East Lothian. In the year 1435 on his arrival in Scotland the Papal legate Aeneas Silvius Piccolomini (who later became Pope Pius II) was shipwrecked near North Berwick, in severe wintry weather. In the course of that visit he wrote home saying that the people of Scotland were very poor, so poor that they did not burn wood, but only a kind of black stone. When the poor people were given a bag of these black stones, they went away very happy. Perhaps the first occasion Piccolomini saw this form of charity was on a winter's day in North Berwick.

Another clue about coal traffic and also perhaps the decay of the passenger ferry comes from a famous account by James Melville, Professor of Hebrew and Oriental Languages at St. Andrews and Minister of Kilrenny, of a crossing from North Berwick in 1586. He says *"We shipped in weil unadvisedly, for the day was very fair, in a mickle coal-boat, wherein was but ane auld man and twa young boys"* *"We hoised sail, with a little pirrhe of east wind, and launched forth until almost a third of the passage was past, and then it fell down dead calm. For rowing, neither was there oars meet, nor hands, the boat was sae heavy, the man auld and the boys young"*. There were five passengers in addition to the crew, and two horses, which would contribute to the weight of the boat; and Robert Durie, Melville's companion, had to help by rowing for three hours. Despite the lack of wind there was a heavy swell, which made four of the passengers sick; and *"the mast shook sae louse that Mr. Robert (the auld man being dammish and machless) had muckle ado to fasten the same"*. A thick haar came in from the east, which produced enough wind (though Melville thought there was no wind at all) to enable sail to be hoisted again and to carry the boat so that *"we arrivit within the Ailie; and, after a maist wearisome and sair day, got a comfortable night's lodging with a godly lady in Carmury"*. Carmury was not far from the present-day farmhouse of Broomlees. The lady with whom he found lodging was the widow of Paul Dishington of Ardross, whose nephew Thomas took the first steps in the building of a regular harbour.

The fact that Melville crossed in a coal boat, presumably returning empty to the Fife side, does not necessarily mean that more conventional ferry boats were not still in use in 1586. He says he and his party "unadvisedly" shipped in a coal boat. This carries the implication that this was a matter of choice on his part. Possibly he did not choose to wait, perhaps meaning the loss of a day, for the conventional ferry. With the great decline in traffic there might be only one boat operating. Wood records that James VI made the crossing in 1592. It seems unlikely that the king would cross in a coal boat, however mickle, but probably he would not have to depend on the public ferry either, though he might have used it.

It was at the period when the ferry service was in steep decline that Thomas Dishington began to develop the Elie Law site for his harbour. One of the factors encouraging him to do so would be the prospect of his commodious harbour with its easy access to the open firth capturing the coal export trade.

THE COCKSTAIL ROCKS LANDING

It is difficult to establish when the narrow creek at the Cockstail Rocks was developed into a mini-harbour (4, 7). One possibility is that at the time Dishington was developing Elie Law, with the decline of the ferry and of the hospital for pilgrims, the burgh of Earlsferry decided to create a second landing under its own control. Under conditions when ships and boats could easily enter Dishington's new harbour but would not dare to attempt the rockbound ferry inlet, the open entrance from the firth to the Cockstail Rocks, even though the harbour itself was narrow, would be of service. Earlsferry fishermen would be reluctant to pay dues, which would cost them a proportion of their catch, to the laird of Ardross; and their manoeuvrable small boats would be able, skilfully handled, to enter the Cockstail Rocks harbour under most conditions good enough for them to go to sea at all. There are indications in later accounts that this harbour was also used for coal exports at one time.

5

Development in the troubled seventeenth century

The 16th century had been a period of great change in the fortunes of Elie and Earlsferry. The end of the pilgrim traffic was in due course to prove fatal to the ferry, and had before the end of the century already done great damage to the prosperity of Earlsferry. The hospice at Chapel Ness had lost its raison d'être and no doubt also the income from the endowments that had supported it. Earlsferry had what might have been a valuable asset, the trading status of a royal burgh, which conferred important trading monopolies, but it was not accepted as a member of the Convention of Royal Burghs, because they believed Earlsferry could not pay its share of the "*Extents*", the taxation imposed on the royal burghs by Parliament; and its charter did not include a defined area of trading monopoly.

In exercising their rights the guild brethren of Earlsferry had severe difficulties to overcome, particularly the lack of a large local market. There was strong competition near at hand from the other royal burghs of East Fife, dominated by Crail, long-established as a trading centre. Pittenweem was also a close competitor. The scale of the old street frontages to be seen in both burghs compares interestingly with Earlsferry's single old street. The merchants of the burgh needed capital to finance their trade, not so easy to raise when the cash flow generated by the pilgrim traffic had ceased, together with the demands of the pilgrims for supplies of all kinds, including the imported goods in which the royal burghs had trading advantages. In earlier years, as we have seen, there is evidence of ships from England trading at Earlsferry. However, as ships engaged in overseas trade grew larger the severe limitations of Earlsferry's two small harbours must have restricted the port's capacity to handle overseas trade. Fishing boats and small vessels engaged in the Scottish coasting trade would be the main users.

We have good information about the size of ships, which would not have changed a great deal over the period, from later in the century. In the 1690s ships engaged in overseas trade entering the port of Dundee averaged 55 tons laden, equivalent to about 80 tons by modern ship measurement. National records of about the same period produce an average of 67 tons, by 17th century measurement, for overseas-owned ships entering Scottish ports. Ships engaged in the coastal trade entering Dundee averaged around 18 tons. Carriage of goods by coastal vessels was of enormous importance. In the 17th century, according to Lythe and Butt "*overland transport, relying mainly on the pack horse, the sledge, or the droving of animals, was ..... a slow and inefficient business. The commercial life of Scotland depended primarily on water transport*".

Except perhaps for the export of fish, small coastal vessels would carry most of the cargoes shipped through the East Fife ports. For the coastal trade in coal Earlsferry had a significant advantage over Elie. Its two harbours were much nearer to the coal mines on the links. Chapman notes that the Cockstail Rocks harbour was used by "*vessels of light burden*" in the days when the Ferry's coal seams were worked. An important factor was that a large part of the coastal trade in coal was to nearby small harbours and other landing places, like the creeks and piers in the estuary of the Tay, as well as small harbours further north. Small coastal vessels (carrying little more coal than a modern lorry) were well adapted to serve these small ports.

The ferry service lasted for some time into the 17th century. There is a specific record of its use in 1600 by a minister on his way home from Teviotdale to Stirling. He had been banned from entering Edinburgh and ten miles round, and using the Earl's ferry enabled him to comply with the ban. In 1621 King James required Scott of Scotstarvit to replace to the same standard elsewhere on his property a part of the road to Cupar from the ferry, which Scott wished to divert from a line which cut between his mansion and its out-buildings. In 1651 the Earl's ferry was described by a travel writer as "*the ferrie near Elie*", which shows that the ferry was still using Earlsferry as its terminal and not the harbour of Elie, but that Elie had become better known. By 1692 it was reported that North Berwick had neither ships nor ferry-boats. After seven centuries or more the ferry had ceased to run, though the fishermen on both sides would occasionally take passengers across and the coal boats would also no doubt do so. The ferry pier continued in use for fishing boats and some cargo shipping.

At the beginning of the century the fortunes of Elie were on the rise. In the 1580s and 1590s, when Dishington and Scott were developing the harbour at Elie Law, substantial houses began to be built in what is now South Street, the Terrace and Rankeillor Street. The Castle, Seafort, Duddingston House, and Wynd House all have their origins in this period. There were others, some now demolished. These merchant houses were not far from the harbour and the point where carts across the sands from the harbour came ashore at the foot of School Wynd. The houses seem to have been built mainly by local landed families, who had the means to afford them and were no doubt seeking to increase the incomes which their small estates yielded by taking part in shipping and mercantile activities. These families were among the beneficiaries of the large investments in the new harbour made by the lairds of Ardross. Younger sons who were successful in trade could obtain estates for themselves by purchase or by marrying heiresses. Landed family names which appear in documents or on tombstones with designations like "*mariner in Elie*" or "*skipper in Elie*" include Dudingston (of Sandford) and Nairne (of Newton Rires). Trading skippers who acquired estates by marriage or purchase include Small (part of Newton Rires now called Charlton) and the best-known and most successful 17th century skipper in Elie, Alexander Gillespie. We can begin to put names to the shipowners of Elie.

Under the peaceful rule of James VI, there was an opportunity lasting several decades for the harbour of Elie to realise the ambitions of its founders, but

there were problems. Elie had the disadvantage of being only a baronial burgh and port, which meant it did not enjoy the trading privileges which were exclusive to the royal burghs, although it had a royal charter which conferred important harbour rights upon the lairds of Ardross. In strict law, only merchant burgesses in royal burghs were authorised to trade with France, Flanders, and other foreign parts, or to sell wine, wax, silk, spices, and similar luxury imports. Foreigners were allowed to buy and sell only within the walls of a royal burgh; and it was only there that fish, wool and hides might be sold to foreigners. All cloth for sale had to be carried to a royal burgh to be finished. The high-water mark of royal burghal monopoly was reached at least in law when these rights were expressly re-stated in an Act of 1633. Throughout the century (whenever political conditions permitted) the royal burghs attempted to emphasise and enforce these rights; but they had great difficulty in enforcing them, particularly over ports belonging to important noblemen and influential landowners like the lairds of Ardross. At the end of the century the royal burghs agreed a compromise on "*the communication of trade*" which shared the rights with other burghs in return for a contribution of ten per cent towards the land tax the royal burghs had to pay. Elie was one of the burghs assessed for a tiny part of this contribution. Pryde notes that "*until well on in the eighteenth century, many 'unfree traders' preferred, to the grandiose plan of 'communication of trade', the simpler and more profitable device of what was, in the strict legal sense, smuggling*". The history of smuggling in East Fife did not begin with the imposition of the hated British custom duties, based at English levels, after the Parliamentary Union of 1707, but had a much longer history, in which the Elie shore would have its share.

It is not clear how big a part the important coal trade might have played at Elie. There was much competition for the overseas trade in coal from good harbours close to the mines further up the Forth, as well as from Pittenweem. From as early as 1480 "*steinkolen*" - coal - begins to appear in the Dutch records; and by the early 1600s it is reported that scores of Dutch ships were being loaded in the Forth ports. The records of the port of Veere, where the "*Scottish staple*" (the privileged centre for Scottish trade to the Netherlands) was located, show in some years the arrival of as many as fifty colliers from Scotland, which means the coal ports of the Forth. Because coal was such a heavy and bulky cargo much of it would necessarily be shipped to other continental ports nearer the points of consumption, indicating that this figure would have to be multiplied a good deal to get the total numbers of shipments, perhaps amounting to five or ten a week. With a fine new harbour not far from the mines on Earlsferry links and others not far away belonging to the Earl of Balcarres at Colinsburgh and Rires, it seems likely that Elie would have a share in that trade. Coal was one of the cargoes listed in Sir John Anstruther's schedule of shore dues of 1740, though in the period between 1663 and 1685 Alexander Gillespie, an Elie skipper who frequently carried coal to the continent, does not record loading coal at Elie. Outward-bound ships would also carry other cargoes. Salt was an important export from Pittenweem; and it is also mentioned in Sir John's schedule. There had been salt-pans near Kincraig in the Middle Ages. The most important Scottish exports were still fish, skins, wool-fells, wool, with some linen cloth and knitted hose the principal manufactured exports. The fertile lands around Elie, much of which was owned by the owners of the harbour and the lairds interested in shipping, would produce some surplus grain for shipping from the harbour.

In the first half of the century a varying proportion of the trade of the Forth was carried on in foreign ships. Dutch ships coming to load coal and returning Scottish colliers would carry imports. The illustration (6) shows the rig of a typical Dutch-built ship of the period. Famously, the characteristic pan-tiles of the east coast of Scotland were first imported from Holland, though later manufactured at home. This heavy paying cargo was a very suitable form of ballast for ships that carried coal, and there was a local demand for tiles in and near the coal ports. Norwegian ships carried timber, and Baltic ships and ships from the Hanseatic towns carried mixed cargoes. For timber there was considerable demand in areas around the Fife ports.

More valuable cargoes from the Low Countries included small manufactures ranging from stationery to weapons and household fitments and equipment, soap, spices, fruits, onions, dyestuffs and textiles. Because of the limited market served by Elie, ships from there bringing back these

more sophisticated cargoes would commonly land most of these valuable goods at ports further up the Forth, particularly Leith, but also Bo'ness for goods destined for central Scotland and Glasgow. In times of scarcity ships, coming from the Baltic ports, especially Danzig, brought grain, shipped down the Vistula from the extensive grain-lands of Poland and the Ukraine. Danzig was also a source of timber, and an entrepot where bar iron from Sweden and commodities like flax and resin could be obtained. Ships from the Forth sailed to Bordeaux for wine, but this cargo was mostly landed at Leith, with small quantities landed at smaller ports for local consumption.

PEACEFUL DEVELOPMENT DISRUPTED

The peaceful development of commerce and industry suffered severe setbacks around the middle of the century. A number of events affecting Elie Harbour at that time can be understood only in the context of the revolution that transformed the life of Scotland in a way similar to what happened in the Reformation in the middle of the previous century. At intervals, political, religious, economic and social life was disrupted by periods of great and sometimes violent unrest, including civil war. Charles I succeeded his father in 1625, and his highly unpopular initiatives in religious matters eventually brought about an extremely complex revolution in Scotland, one of the major factors that helped to bring about the English Civil War. These national events caused great disturbances particularly over the period from 1639, when open warfare first broke out, briefly, in Aberdeenshire, to 1660 when Charles II was restored to the throne of Great Britain. Even under the relatively peaceful Cromwellian inter-regnum from 1651 to 1660. Fife was not free from military disturbances. There were lesser disturbances after 1660 in the reigns of Charles II and James VII and II, ending in 1688 with the lasting revolutionary settlement under William and Mary.

Perhaps surprisingly, it was in this troubled period that the first lighthouse on the Isle of May was erected. Permission was granted in 1636 to two landowners to levy an impost on ships for the purpose of erecting and maintaining a light on the May, which permission was ratified by Parliament in 1641. The right to the impost was confirmed to Sir John Cunninghame of Barnes in East Lothian by Parliament in 1645 in terms which make it clear that by that date the light had been erected and was already in operation. The impost was four shillings (Scots) equal to four pence sterling per ton burden for foreign vessels and two shillings for home vessels hailing from all ports between Dunottar on the north and St. Abbs Head on the south. The light was produced by burning a ton of coal a night, in a chauffer or iron cage beacon, which after 1656 was on top of a tower (8), initially forty feet high but latterly raised to sixty feet.

The parliamentary forces, dominated by the Covenanting party opposed to the king's religious measures, had the upper hand in the small military actions in Aberdeenshire in 1639. This led Charles I to muster substantial forces in England to over-awe the Scots. These included a fleet of nineteen ships under the Duke of Hamilton, doubtfully alleged to be carrying five thousand soldiers, which entered the Forth on 1 May 1639. All of the towns of the Forth coast fortified themselves and mustered their forces to ward off the threat of invasion. At this stage in the dispute many who later supported the Stuart kings, ultimately at great personal cost, helped to form the Scottish regiments that opposed his forces. The great Montrose had a regiment of 1500 men in the Covenanting army. There were at least two full regiments from Fife, under the leadership of the noble families of Rothes, Lindsay and Sinclair. In face of this English threat to the Scottish Parliament, which was in negotiations with the king, Lord Balcarres raised a troop of horse for the Parliament, despite being a staunch royalist. In the event this conflict was avoided and there were no landings on the Forth; but the state of alarm which led so many in Fife, as elsewhere, to take up arms was an ominous foretaste of worse things to come.

Among these disasters, the heaviest losses for Fife were those suffered at the battle of Kilsyth in August 1644 by the Fife regiments including one drawn mainly from East Fife, which must have included some men from Elie and Earlsferry. In greatly changed circumstances, Montrose was now supporting the king against the Covenanting establishment. At Kilsyth his army of Highlanders and Irishmen inflicted a savage defeat on the Lowland regiments they opposed. A royalist source said boastfully that no unmounted covenanter escaped alive from the battle. The thriving town

of Pittenweem sent two hundred men to the Parliamentary army, of whom only five returned alive. This did considerable damage for a time to the town's fishing industry and other productive activities. The losses from Elie and Earlsferry would be much less. The royalist sympathies of Scott of Ardross, Wood of Grange and other local lairds would have limited the recruitment to the Fife regiments from the Elie area.

Occasional glimpses of unusual events at Elie Harbour during this troubled period are to be found both in Wood and in John Lamont's diary. John Lamont's identity remains in doubt. He may have belonged to a landowning family in the Leven area. The published version of his diary covers the period from 1649 to 1671. He tries to give some account of the most notable events in Scotland, and particularly in Fife, during that period. Events arising from the religious strife, great civil disturbances, and military conflict are naturally prominent in Lamont's record.

Following his defeat in the English Civil War and a long period of political intrigues, Charles I had been executed in London in January 1649. Shortly afterwards, the Scots Parliament proclaimed his son Charles II, then in exile in Holland, to be King of Great Britain, France and Ireland; but they attached conditions to his return to the throne. This entailed much coming and going between Scotland and Holland. Wood records that the royalist Earls of Lauderdale and Lanark (later to be Duke of Hamilton) had arrived in Elie harbour one morning, not long before the king's execution, in a Flemish man-of-war in which Lauderdale had come over from Holland. Lord Balcarres, a royalist, now at odds with the Covenanting forces dominating Scotland, had come down to Elie to confer on board the ship with his two friends. Lauderdale and Lanark did not linger, for they feared arrest at the behest of the Scottish Parliament, but sailed for safety in Holland in the afternoon. Lauderdale left behind his precious charter chest, which Balcarres took back for safe-keeping to be buried in his courtyard. When the chest was recovered after the Restoration in 1661 water penetration had made many of the documents illegible.

Wood also records a slightly later frustrated attempt by a local nobleman to flee to Holland. *Some months after, the earl of Crawford and Lindsay, being threatened with imprisonment because he would not acknowledge the lawfulness of the last session of Parliament, resolved also to escape to Holland, and repaired to Elie with the intention of embarking; but commissioners having been sent to seize all his property his lady sent to the Ely for him and caused him to return home."*

In defiance of the English Parliament, the Scottish Parliament reached a concordat with Charles II and he was duly crowned at Scone on 1 January 1651. This brought about a Cromwellian invasion. While the Cromwellians were over-running Scotland later that year a Scottish frigate captured an English supply ship in the Forth and brought her into Elie. The ship's load of biscuit was handed over to the Scottish army, then in the last stages of its unavailing attempts to defeat the invasion. Later that same year, after capturing Burntisland, Cromwellian cavalry came along the coast and made a prize of a ship in Elie Harbour belonging to John Small.

Lamont records that in 1654, Royalist forces in the north of Scotland sent parties into Fife to commandeer horses, taking away the best that they could find. In late December they came to Elie, and collected five horses in the parish, three of them from Dudingston of Sandford (now St. Ford). The commandeering of the best horses (later by both sides) must have had a damaging effect on many aspects of life, including the haulage of goods to and from harbours, mitigated a little by the continuing use of draught oxen - of no use to cavalrymen - at this period. Following the Royalist raids the Cromwellian commander in Scotland ordered that all horses worth more than £5 were to be surrendered to the nearest garrison, where they would be valued and paid for. These orders were enforced by searches and confiscations, and many horses were surrendered to the garrison at Falkland.

The very damaging effects of the continuing unrest are described in the diary of John Nicoll, an Edinburgh lawyer, writing about the year 1654. *"This yeir, also the povertie of the land daylie increst, be reason of the inlaik (deficiency) of tred and traffick, both be sea and land, the pepill being poore and under cess (taxation), quarterings (billeting of soldiers), and uther burdinges... Sindrie of gude rank, alsweill nobles, gentrie, and burgessis, denuncit to the horne, thair escheittis (property forfeited) takin, thair persones wairdit*

and imprissoned, and detenit thairin till thair death. Bankruptes and brokin men throw all the pairtes of the natioun increst"

These conditions extended to *"all the pairtes of the natioun"*. Elie would not be exempt; but in the middle of the Cromwellian interregnum it is recorded that in 1655, when Thomas Tucker's census of Scottish shipping states that in the whole of Scotland there were only 80 ships above 25 tons burden, the ports of Elie and Leven each had two vessels. Those of Leven were 20 tons and 18 tons, and those of Elie 40 tons and 50 tons. The entrepreneurial shipmasters of Elie were still active. Perhaps the two Elie ships included a replacement for the ship belonging to John Small which had been taken as a prize by Cromwell's soldiers in 1651: or perhaps Small had been able to buy it back. These Elie ships were of about average size for vessels engaged in overseas trade across the North Sea. This does not imply that they traded overseas from Elie, since at that time the home port of a ship simply meant the port where the ship's skipper lived; but it does show that Elie had become a base for the shipping trade.

In that same year the inhabitants of Elie must have had a serious fright, not recorded by Wood or Lamont. The President of the Cromwellian Council in Scotland had complained of the lack of a warship to protect the shipping in the Forth. His complaints were shown to be well justified when in 1656 Dunkirk privateers entered the Forth and raided the shipping there. A manuscript in Worcester College, Oxford, noted by F.D. Dow, records that these marauders came ashore at Elie in July 1656. Probably they needed water and other stores, and would look for other booty too. It was obviously not a major raid, for it is not recorded by Lamont who had a keen eye for calamities of any kind. Presumably the two Elie ships were not at home to be taken in prize, for Lamont undoubtedly would have reported that, as he reported the taking of Small's ship in 1651.

ELIE AS A HARBOUR OF REFUGE

An important area of interest for Lamont was the damage inflicted by storms; and it is significant of the shelter afforded by Elie harbour that despite severe problems in other nearby harbours he reports little or no damage at Elie. He reports a severe storm on Dec. 10 1655 which did great damage in the harbours of Fife, even breaking down the piers in "*St. Andrews, Enster, Craill and Weymes*". A total of 50 ships were sunk in Enster, Dysart and Craill. He reports no damage at Elie. In June 1659 an English vessel laden with salt was torn from its moorings in "Leith rode", ran for shelter to Elie harbour, but sank there. All the crew were saved.

Lamont records three further storms in 1669, on Sept. 17, Sept. 24 and Oct. 13. Despite serious losses elsewhere there appears to have been none worth mentioning at Elie; but Elie again figures as a place to seek refuge. "*Also, Sept. 24, ...a ship belonging to Preston Pans in Lowthian came downe from London, richly laden with divers commodities, and rich merchant goods, being in the Firth some days before, fearing a tempest also, lowsed with a purpose to go for the Elly, mistaking the harbour, sett in above the Ferry upon the rocks at Kincraig and perished. The men were safe, and many of the goods recovered; bot the countrey peopell paryet (preyed) upon many of them (i.e. the goods). Upon which James Mitchell, skipper, and some others that had interest, procwred ane order from the chanclowr, the Er. Of Rothes, for restitution of the goods, which was read Oct. 3, 1669, in several churches after sermon, as in Largo, Newburne, Kilconqr., etc., to be delivered back to the skipper, or in his absence to John Whytt, skipper in the Elly, and somewhat promised to such as browght back any thing.*" Lamont does not report any ships that ran safely for Elie, perhaps, like any modern journalist, seeking out the more sensational events for his record. He does show that Elie was coming to be regarded as a harbour of refuge.

EVENTS AFTER THE RESTORATION OF 1660

The Cromwellian interregnum ended in 1660 with the proclamation of Charles II as King on May 8 and his return to London on May 29. On June 12, the body of the Earl of Balcarres was solemnly buried at Balcarres. He had died in exile in Holland in September, 1659, and his remains had been landed at Elie in December; but his funeral did not take place till after the King's restoration.

There is a typical passage in Lamont recording the return of another member of a local landowning family by way of Elie harbour. "*1661, Mar. 20 John Woods corps were landed in the Ellie, which were browght downe from London, by John Whyte,*

skipper ther. He was a cadet of the house of Largo, and it was he that caused build the stone dyke about the church of Largo and buelt the schole house at Rameldrie. They were interred in Largo Iylle the 22 of July 1661, being Moneday, in the day tyme. He appointed also a Hospitall to be built at Largo, for honest persons that decayed in their substance." Wood's account of this event also records that there was some opposition in the family to the burial in the family vault, and that in consequence the body lay in Elie church from 20 March to 22 July.

After the periods of exile earlier endured in the Low Countries by royalist supporters it is perhaps not surprising that after 1660 there were corresponding experiences for the other side. In 1663 Covenanting ministers and others who would not submit to Episcopal government of the church found safety by leaving Scotland for Holland, which seems to have been the favourite destination for asylum-seekers from both sides. Lamont records various comings and goings, and also journeys to London by sea: - "*in Apr. Mr. George Younger, m. of Newburn, took shipping for London; he went off at the earls ferry to a Kirkcaldie vessel*". It was cheaper and easier to get to London from East Fife by sea rather than by road.

Curiously, despite his interest in reporting dramatic events, Lamont does not record one of the most frightening passages in the naval history of the Forth at this period. There must have been great alarm at Elie and on both sides of the Forth on the last day of April 1667, when in the course of Charles II's disastrous war against the Dutch, 30 ships of their fleet under Admiral Van Ghent came up the estuary as far as Burntisland. The second Earl of Wemyss recorded in his diary that the Dutch ships fired over 1000 cannon shot at the town, but were beaten off and did not succeed in landing. The big ships of the Royal Navy in the south had all been laid up because the Admiralty had run out of money and in consequence the Dutch had the free run of the North Sea. The three Royal Navy ships riding in Leith Roads at the time had been withdrawn to run for safety above the Queensferry narrows, defended by the artillery fort on Inchgarvie. Fortunately, the Dutch fleet left the Forth the next day, and, according to Wemyss "*did littill more than tuek one privatirre belonging to Leith, Shoe ridding in Brunelland Rode when they cam up*". It was later that season that the Dutch

6. Tombstone carving of Fife merchant ship - 1672

7. Fisherman at Cockstail Rocks c.1940

8. The first lighthouse on the Isle of May

9. The Royal yacht *Portsmouth* - 1674

inflicted a disgraceful defeat on the Royal Navy by entering the Medway and burning or taking away the best of the great laid-up ships that had been the pride of the Navy.

ALEXANDER GILLESPIE – MERCHANT
SHIPOWNER

Whereas in the early part of the century a varying proportion - sometimes quite a lot - of the overseas trade of the Scottish ports was carried on in foreign-owned vessels, after 1660 Scottish-owned ships, some with foreign partners among the owners, dominated the trade. The 17th century Elie merchant skipper about whom we have the most information was Alexander Gillespie, the reason being that he kept a journal of his voyages. At least part of it, covering the years from 1662 to 1685, survives in the custody of St. Andrews University Library, together with a very helpful transcription and some notes by Paula Martin. The text begins at 14 April 1662 when Gillespie returned to Elie from Holland, and breaks off as abruptly as it began on 31 July 1685 with him recording that his ship was detained at Brill on the Dutch coast near Rotterdam - he does not state the reason. Elie was Gillespie's base, from which he regularly took his departure for his overseas voyages, and which he usually made his first port of call on his return. He does not specifically record loading or unloading at Elie; but one or two voyages appear to have ended in Elie with no reference to unloading there or elsewhere, and this suggests that he may on occasion have unloaded, for example with timber from Norway, at his home port.

There can be no doubt that he would land some imported goods at Elie for his family and friends and for the local trade, and he would pay the appropriate "*shore dues*" for anything landed in this way. He would also be liable to pay landing dues for himself and his crew, and harbour dues for his ship, which would make his contribution to the finances of the harbour significant. Before departing on a long voyage to the continent he would purchase and load most of his ship's stores locally, requiring fair quantities for his longer voyages, for example to Bordeaux. He records "*dressing*" his ship at Elie after unloading at Leith following a stormy passage from Bordeaux, which suggests that his ships were normally maintained

at his home base. It also seems likely that most if not all of his crew were Elie men. The journal does not contain details of his ship, the *Anna*, which he used for much of the period, but we know that she could carry a cargo of 85 tons.

The fine ship carving in the photograph (6) is on the tombstone of Robert Ford of Kilrenny, who died in 1672, and shows the rig of a typical merchant ship of the period. Colin Martin has noted that "The vessel shows the distinctive characteristics of a Dutch fluit, and is apparently unarmed. A navigational cross-staff is shown on the right while the circle on the left probably represents a mariner's compass". Many of the ships sailed by Scottish skippers were built in Holland.

It appears that most if not all of the cargoes Gillespie carried to London or overseas were loaded at other east coast ports. Coal and salt were common cargoes for him. On at least one occasion he loaded coal at Cockenzie, where the enterprising Cadells had an efficient integrated business, mining, transporting and exporting coal from their own harbour, no doubt at highly competitive prices. On one occasion in 1668 he carried 85 tons of coal from Dysart to London where it was sold at prices ranging from 17s to 20s per ton, which would mean in total about 950 pounds Scots. He loaded salt at Methil and Dysart, and corn at Newburgh and perhaps elsewhere in the Tay estuary. He loaded herring at Stornoway (to which he carried salt), Lochinver and Lerwick.

His journal is a record chiefly of the passages he made, and does not give an account of his cargoes though some are occasionally mentioned. Bulky cargoes like wine, timber, flax, and dried peas are mentioned, and also bar iron from Sweden, purchased in Danzig, where he usually sold salt. In England he landed cargoes in London and Yarmouth. In Holland he sailed to Amsterdam and Rotterdam with coal. He regularly went to Norway for timber, usually on the second leg of a triangular voyage taking in a port like Rotterdam. In France he sailed to Dieppe on one occasion carrying troops. He went regularly to Bordeaux for wine, and once for the same cargo to Nantes.

The best information we have about the cargoes he imported comes from the Customs House books of Leith, the regular landing place for his wine cargoes from Bordeaux and mixed cargoes of merchant goods, from London in particular.

He sometimes made two voyages to Bordeaux to purchase wine from one vintage, one in the late autumn and the other at the beginning of the year, calling at Elie on his return before going on to Leith to land his cargo. Winter conditions did not prevent him from making these long and exposed voyages, though he was sometimes delayed by stormy weather, and on one or two occasions briefly detained in the Channel by privateers whom he had to buy off.

There is no record in the customs books of the quantities of wine Gillespie brought into Leith; but the wine cargo usually took several days to load in Bordeaux. Clearly he carried a lot. The next largest cargo from Bordeaux was prunes, followed by vinegar. In April 1675 he landed at Leith 5,400 pounds of prunes, 6 hogsheads of vinegar, 2,300 pounds of French tobacco, 12 barrels of walnuts, 400 pounds of ham, 140 pounds of dry confections, and 80 pounds of soap. In April 1681, after being long detained at the mouth of the Gironde by gales, and a slow passage to Elie lasting from 1 to 31 March, his landings at Leith included 9000 pounds of prunes. In other years he also brought from Bordeaux brandy, chestnuts and paper.

Perhaps not surprisingly, the most varied cargo landed by Gillespie at Leith came from London. In April 1674 his London shipment included cloths of several kinds (silk, fine broadcloth, coarse broadcloth, flannel and freize) as well as skins, raw silk, made clothes, and linen goods; haberdashery, shoemakers ware and shoemakers "*culler*"; hawk bells, hawk lures, and hawk hoods; paper, galls (for making ink), dyestuffs, gum "*arabeck*", and "*indicol*"; furniture, a clock, a looking glass, candlesticks, cutlery, wrought pewter, and whiting; tools for several trades, wire, and huge quantities of barrel hoops; a barrel of whisky; "*hopps*", tobacco, raisins, "*figgs*", West India ginger and cheeses.

In the 24 years covered by his journal Gillespie made 65 voyages and his affairs clearly prospered. In July 1676 he was at Rotterdam, contracting with a shipbuilder for a new ship for which he returned in January 1677. On 18 January of that year he took his departure from Brill in his new ship, recording her name in the journal as "*The Jeams*", a variant of James. She could carry a cargo of 120 tons. Later he was able to build a grand house in South Street, known as "*The Muckle Yett*", of which a substantial ghost remains, much altered

and reduced in scale, with a fine carved doorway hinting at former grandeur. The doorway bears the date 1685, and, in accordance with custom, Gillespie's initials and those of his wife Christian Small. Wood supposes Christian to be of the same family as John Small, the ship-owner. It is clear she took an active part in her husband's business affairs. One of John Small's daughters was married to James Nairne, skipper of Elie. The sea-faring families in Elie were a close-knit group. The Smalls are commemorated in two stones in the churchyard, with the effigy of a ship, one bearing the date 1678. Alexander Gillespie's grave is marked by a grand finely-carved tombstone near the churchyard gate, but there is no ship carving to commemorate his notable maritime career.

A ROYAL YACHT AT ELIE

It was in Gillespie's fine house in South Street that the brother of Charles II, James Duke of York, later to be King James VII and II, stayed when he came to Elie in his yacht. James had been sent to Edinburgh in December 1679, to be the King's Lord High Commissioner, a kind of Viceroy, presiding over the Scottish Privy Council which governed the country. King Charles wanted him out of England, where the Protestant mob caused problems for the Catholic Duke, who was the heir to the throne. Though the power of the Presbyterian establishment had been broken and temporarily replaced by a more compliant Episcopalian hierarchy, Protestant Edinburgh would not be much more welcoming, and James would be pleased to escape to Elie where he could visit royalist friends like the Earl of Balcarres and Sir William Anstruther. It is interesting that he chose to lodge independently in a rich merchant skipper's house rather than stay in an aristocratic house. Perhaps Gillespie's large modern house was more luxurious and better adapted to the Duke's way of life; and no doubt the household would be at his command, rather more so than if he was a guest - even though a royal one - in an aristocratic grandee's house.

The harbour in which the Duke's yacht berthed is clearly delineated in a map entitled "*The East Part of Fife surveyed and designed be John Adair Math. 1684*". On a scale of about one inch to the mile, it clearly shows the three structures that made up the harbour of Elie as built by Dishington and finished off by Scott around 1600. These are the swarf dyke, the quay and the pier, which are shown forming three straight lines enclosing "*Ely port*" marked with a symbolic anchor. Of the three other East Neuk harbours shown only Anstruther is so marked, perhaps suggesting these were the only suitable places for ships looking for shelter, with the estuary of the Dreel burn at Anstruther and the wide entrance to Elie harbour offering much easier entry than any of the other harbours.

The first recorded yacht in Elie Harbour was a very splendid one. When Charles II returned from exile in Holland in 1660 he brought with him a finely-appointed yacht, the *Mary,* the gift of the Dutch East India Company. She was of 100 tons burden, had a crew of thirty, and carried eight guns. With that yacht, and others built in Holland and in England, Charles and James introduced the English aristocracy to the pleasures of yachting and yacht racing. The yacht in which James visited Elie was called the *Anne* after his duchess, and was a fairly close copy of the *Mary*, with the same war-like complement of eight guns. Both yachts were formally part of the Royal Navy, in which respect the royal brothers were again following Dutch practice. By the 1670s fair numbers of yachts had been built for the royal family and their friends.

These yachts were modelled on the *Mary*, a gaff-rigged cutter; the Dutch were the recognised masters of ship design. A good impression of what the residents of Elie saw when the *Anne* entered the harbour is given by the illustration (9) showing the *Portsmouth*, taken from a painting by Van de Velde the Elder. The *Portsmouth*, named after the Duchess of Portsmouth who was one of Charles's mistresses, was built for the king in 1674, and was large enough to have ports for at least 12 guns.

The *Anne* would not be allowed into Elie Harbour today, given her dimensions: - Length of keel 52 feet: Breadth 19 feet: Draught 7 feet.

Probably the most unusual cargo loaded at Elie Harbour was one transported to Leith in the Duke's yacht. In the course of the yacht's visits to Elie the Duke's coxswain succeeded in courting the daughter of Thomas Turnbull of Bogmill, a landowner. According to the received story recounted by Wood they were surreptitiously married by the Episcopal minister of Kilconquhar, Dr. William Hay; and the bride was smuggled out of the harbour in the yacht in an open-topped barrel covered by a cloth, alleged to contain a swan from Kilconquhar Loch, being transported to improve the breed of swans on St. Margaret's Loch, near Holyrood Palace, the Duke of York's vice-regal residence. Turnbull was enraged that his daughter had married a common sailor, and had to be bought off by the Duke. Wood prints a song which was written about this romantic episode.

OTHER SHIP OWNERS
There is some information about one or two other ship owners of this period who were based at Elie Harbour. Gillespie records that on 18 February 1665 he sailed from Elie for Rotterdam in company with Robert Nairne in his Elie ship. Robert Nairne was a successful merchant skipper. Christopher Smout records the name of his ship, *Anna of Elie* (which he may have bought from Gillespie), and that between 1680 and 1686 he sailed between Leith and Bordeaux, London, Holland, Danzig, Konigsberg, and Norway. Clearly he was engaging in the same kind of trade as Gillespie. His prosperity was such as to enable him to lend substantial sums to the Scott family of Ardross. In 1697 he is recorded as lending, in two tranches, a total of about £500 Scots to one of the Scott daughters; and in 1706 he bought another Scott bond of 1686 for £230 Scots. Among earlier lenders to the Scotts we find Margaret Wood, relict of Peter Nairn, skipper in Elie, and also one Heggie, skipper in Elie. The merchant skippers of Elie had cash to spare.

There is one small group of skippers of this period of whom we know at least their names and that they took part in herring fishing. Those who took part in the drave, the pursuit of the migrating shoals of herring, were registered with the Admiralty Court of East Fife, sitting in the "*Tolbuith of Craill*". The Court's records for the 1690s are to be found in the Scottish Record Office. In 1690 the list of "*dreavers*" contains a considerable number of East Neuk names, but only 4 from Earlsferry and none from Elie. Most were from Anstruther, Crail, Pittenweem, and St. Monans. In 1691 the lists appear to be incomplete, with names only in the spaces headed Crail and Anstruther, and other labelled spaces left blank. In 1692 the lists of "*dreave*" boats included the names of 3 skippers from Anstruther and one from Elie. Earlsferry was at that time and continued to be a substantially more important fishing centre than Elie.

THE ESTATE CHANGES HANDS

These loans to the Scotts of Ardross represented only a tiny part of the indebtedness into which this once wealthy family fell over the period between the 1640s and the 1690s. Supporting the Stuart kings through thick and thin had cost them a great deal of money. Their earlier loans were granted on bonds secured over their extensive estates. By 1677 the Scott titles were so heavily encumbered that legal actions had begun to transfer the estates to other hands. Over the period from 1640 to the 1690s the total borrowings of William Scott and his heirs amounted to over £200,000 Scots. By 1697 all the Scott estates had passed to Sir William Anstruther, all the other creditors having been bought out by him.

REPAIRS TO THE HARBOUR

Scott's straitened finances, and the confused state of the ownership of Ardross and Elie from about 1664 had dire effects on the harbour, by then over 60 years old. The structures erected at the beginning of the century had been allowed to fall into such disrepair as to lead to the submission of a petition for help to the Privy Council on behalf of the burgh and the users of the harbour. In 1696, this petition, signed by William Reid, bailie in Elie, and James and Robert Nairne, skippers there, said *"that the ruinous condition of the harbour of the Elie is witnessed by a certificate, under the hands of several skippers of the burghs of Pittenweem, Anstruther, and Earlsferry: that the harbour is well known to be the securest refuge when ships are put from their anchors in Leith roads: and that it is notour that 300 of his majesty's soldiers had been lost, had it not been for the convenience and safety of that harbour"*. Not for the first or the last time, the harbour's value as a harbour of refuge was being used to make the case for support for its maintenance. The Privy Council's deliverance upon the petition did not offer any help from the Exchequer, but decided to *"allow a volunteer contribution to be made at all the parish churches within this kingdom, for the reparation of the said harbour of the Elie…"*.

Whether the church collections produced substantial funds or not, it appears the harbour was put in good repair, for in 1710 Sir Robert Sibbald's account of the excellence of the harbour made no reference to disrepair. This could well have been one of the benefits of the change of ownership in 1697. The new owner, Sir William Anstruther, was a man of wealth and influence. He had been a member of the Scots Parliament at the time when the Duke of York was Lord High Commissioner for his brother Charles II. At that time he had frequently been in opposition to the measures of the Court, and he supported the Revolution that brought William and Mary to the throne in 1688. In 1689 he became a Judge of the Court of Session and Lord of Justiciary, and he was created a baronet in 1694.

NATIONAL BACKGROUND AT THE END OF THE CENTURY

The national background in the last decade of the century was gloomy. In the seven years from 1695 to 1702 there had been a run of exceptionally bad seasons for Scottish farmers, characterised by blight and famine. Prices of provisions rose to extortionate levels; and many people died from lack of food. If there was any grain surplus in the Elie area for shipping to Edinburgh it would fetch very high prices. The failure in the same period of the ambitious Darien scheme to plant a trading colony on the narrow isthmus of Central America had caused the loss, on a contemporary estimate, of about one-fifth of the available liquid capital of Scotland. There was great discontent with the part King William's English government had played in relation to the Darien scheme and other matters affecting Scotland. The discontent and the harsh conditions of the time were important factors in bringing about the great changes in political thought about relations between Scotland and England that made the Parliamentary Union of 1707 possible.

6
Peaceful progress and civil war

TRADE OF THE BURGHS

By the beginning of the 18th century Earlsferry's harbour trade had greatly diminished. One source says that the burgh had no trade at all, although in 1708 there was still enough activity for a public roup of the Anchorages and Customs (the harbour dues and other local dues on trade in the burgh) to produce a bid of £5 6s 8d for the right to collect these dues. The council minutes record that the successful bid was made "at the outrunning of the glass", that is to say that it was the last bid to be made before a sand-glass inverted at the beginning of the auction had run out. There is later evidence that some use continued to be made of the ferry pier for the export of farm produce, coal, fish for the Edinburgh market, and later, ironstone. As late as 1858 ironstone cargoes from the mine on Earlsferry links were loaded at the pier for shipping to Newcastle.

In 1709 the roup of the dues fetched £7 16s 8d. They were significant contributions to the burgh's meagre finances; but the ending of the ferry had cost the burgh much larger sums. From the outset the burgh's serious disadvantages as a trading centre had been compounded by the refusal of the Convention of Royal Burghs to accept Earlsferry as a member. In 1707/08 the Convention's stance meant that Earlsferry did not receive any share of the Equivalent, the payment made by the English Exchequer to Scotland ostensibly to compensate for the share of the National Debt of England that would thenceforward be borne by Scotland as an integral part of the United Kingdom.

In 1700 Elie made a last throw in the largely ineffectual scheme for the "communication of trade" under which trade privileges would be granted to non-royal burghs in return for money contributions to the Convention's tax burdens. Elie offered eightpence annually in response to an assessment of one shilling and sixpence (a penny half penny sterling). This was rejected as too small; and in 1705 the Convention protested that Elie should not receive the privileges enjoyed by the

royal burghs. Before long the distinction ceased to be of much importance, with the enormous changes introduced by the Union of 1707 and the continuing widespread evasion of the rules. However the pattern of trade between the Forth ports and the continent that had already been set partly by the location of the privileged royal burghs continued, and Elie-owned ships delivered most of their continental cargoes to other ports, principally Leith.

Writing in 1710, Sir Robert Sibbald, "*an eminent physician, naturalist and antiquary*", said in his history of Fife that Elie Harbour was most convenient and safe. "*The water in it at spring tides is twenty-two foot deep. A little to the east there might be a harbour might be made for ships of the greatest burden, and in which lesser ships might enter at low water and be as safe as the other*".

THE ANSTRUTHER LAIRDS

Sir William Anstruther, the owner of Elie Harbour, had been able to enlarge his estates and he enjoyed valuable royal appointments. In the debates in the Scottish Parliament leading up to the union of the Parliaments in 1707 he was one of the Squadrone Volante, the block of floating voters, whose support had to be obtained by whatever means were necessary to carry the vote for the Union. The surveyors of the Ordnance Survey were told by the local informants they consulted in 1853 that the handsome stone obelisk in the field to the south-east of Elie House had been erected to commemorate the Union, presumably by Sir William.

Sir William presided as Admiral in the Admiralty Court of East Fife, an office mainly discharged by his Admiral Depute. He held through his succession to the Scott Charters of Elie "*the office of Searching of all prohibited and uncustomed goods coming to or going from the said Burgh or Port of Elie loaded or unloaded thereat with full power to search for arrest and apprehend the said prohibited and uncustomed goods and merchandice and to intromit therewith as escheat to Her Majesty the one half thereof to pertain to Her Majesty and her successors and the other half to the proprietor of the said Barony as perpetual and heritable Searcher of the said goods and to affix and hold courts one or more for Cognition and trial of the said prohibited and uncustomed goods, and to decide and determine in the said Courts as accords of the Law; as also with power of having a cocquet with the privilege of the seal thereof and to create and constitute an Keeper and Clerk of the said cocquet as oft as need bees".*

Sir William would no doubt have wished to be one of the Scottish members in the new United Kingdom Parliament; but in 1707 he was informed by the House of Commons authorities that neither he nor his heirs could sit in the Commons so long as they held the cocquet, as the office was usually known. Clearly this was an office of profit under the Crown. He did not choose to give it up.

By the end of the 17th century, the harbour was under new ownership; it was established as the base for several shipmasters whose import trade went principally to other Forth ports, which for imports from London or Europe usually meant Leith. It was recognised as a secure and valuable harbour of refuge. The scale of its own trade is not easy to ascertain; but there is evidence from the trivial sums mentioned in relation to the "communication of trade" that no one believed the port and burgh had any prospect of developing a substantial trade in goods monopolised by the royal burghs. Smuggling apart, the trade of the town was mainly in goods not restricted by the rights of the royal burghs.

Sir William's ownership of the harbour gave him the right, under the charter of 1601, to levy harbour dues, which the charter said were to be applied to the maintenance of the fabric of the harbour. In 1707 he also obtained from the courts confirmation of the right, presumably by interpretation of the charter, to levy duties, called in a 1740 document the "*toun customes*", on the products and manufactures of the Barony of Elie, and, it appears, on goods brought into Elie for sale and some goods transported out of the burgh. As late as 1842 this right was being exercised and payments were being collected from some traders; but others were disputing the baron's claims and asking for their legal basis to be demonstrated.

Sir William Anstruther died in 1711. The next owner of the harbour was his son Sir John, who

greatly enlarged his inheritance by the acquisition of parts of Newburn, Balchrystie, and Sandford, and the estates of Newark (St. Monans) and Easter Grangemuir. He also brought other estates into the Anstruther family through his marriage to a daughter of the Earl of Hyndford, Lady Margaret Carmichael. He had inherited his father's valuable powers relating to prohibited and uncustomed goods with the right to half the proceeds of their confiscation. This privilege enabled the Crown to enlist the interest of the proprietors of harbours in the suppression of smuggling, which had become a much larger problem in Scotland after 1707 because of the great increase in customs duties to bring them up to the English level.

Sir John died in 1753 and was succeeded by his son, also Sir John, another enterprising laird. By purchase and inheritance he added to his already extensive estates the remaining part of Sandford, Airdrie, the Kellie estates except the castle, and the superiority of Pittenweem. It was this Sir John who married Jenny Faa (anglicé Fall) for whom the Lady's Tower was built. She belonged to an entrepreneurial family in Dunbar, who had joint business interests with Sir John.

Over the course of the century the enterprising Anstruthers made substantial investments in agricultural improvement, in mining, and in the salt works at St. Monans and the harbour of Pittenweem; but it does not appear that they made any substantial investment in Elie Harbour, apart from the erection of the granary at the beginning of the next century. This suggests that the capacity of the harbour as developed by Dishington and Scott around 1600 was adequate for the trade it had to handle. Elie Harbour did not become one of the main fishing centres, despite its suitability and its location on a coast lined with fishing ports. The harbour dues charged by the proprietor, including his right to teind fish, may have been an important factor in deterring fishermen from using the harbour of Elie. It had however become a home port for ships engaged in overseas trade; and a shipyard building vessels of considerable size was established at the Toft.

AN UNUSUAL FERRY CROSSING
Though the regular ferry service had long been discontinued the old ferry route was still sometimes used by travellers hiring local boats to make the

crossing. Chapman tells of an interesting crossing in 1736 by General Sir Philip Anstruther of Airdrie, a small inland estate between Crail and Anstruther. The General was the M.P. for the East Fife Burghs. In a riot in Edinburgh arising from the execution for theft of a Pittenweem smuggler several people had been shot dead by the Town Guard. Its commander, Captain Porteous, had been convicted of murder, but reprieved by the then equivalent of the Home Secretary. There was no longer a Secretary of State for Scotland. A highly organised mob dragged Porteous from the Tollbooth in which he was imprisoned, and lynched him.

Parliament in London was the scene of fierce disputes. General Anstruther was the only Scots M.P. who supported the government in the enactment of limited but humiliating measures to punish the city of Edinburgh. This made him extremely unpopular in Fife, so much so that in returning from Airdrie to London he chose not to use the ferry from Pettycur to Leith, which seems by then to have become the usual route to Edinburgh for Fifers joining the coach to London. It would have been full of hostile Fifers. The General may have feared being thrown overboard: tempers were very high. Instead of going by Pettycur he hired an Earlsferry fishing boat to take him across. *"You fellows are all great smugglers, no doubt?"* said the General to the fishermen. *"Ou aye"* replied one *"but I dinna think we ever smuggled a general afore"*.

THE HARBOURS AND THE JACOBITES

The story of the harbours in Elie Bay in the first half of the 18th century would not be complete without some account of the impact in the area of the attempts in 1708, 1715 and 1745 to restore the Stuart dynasty. In 1708 Queen Anne, the daughter of James VII and II was still on the throne. One aim of most of the many Scots who supported her brother, whom they considered to be James VIII and III (later known as *"the Old Pretender"*), was to reverse the Parliamentary Union of 1707 by recreating a separate Scottish kingdom and Parliament. There were many in Scotland and England who had the wider aim of putting him then or later on the throne of Great Britain. In both 1708 and 1715 the most conspicuous Jacobite in the Elie area was Malcolm of Grange, who had a particularly important part to play in 1708.

The enormous difference between 1708 and the two later risings was that in 1708 Louis XIV committed substantial French military and naval resources to support a rising in Scotland. Part of his motivation came from the great disaster of the battle of Ramillies, the most complete of all Marlborough's victories on the continent. The allied armies (British, Dutch and Danish) captured all 50 of the French cannon, and 80 standards, and the casualties on the two sides were grossly disproportionate. The French Marshal Villars wrote that Ramillies was *"the most shameful, humiliating, and disastrous of defeats"*. French aims in 1708 of course extended well beyond avenging one defeat. In supporting James Louis was trying to weaken Great Britain by *"playing the Scottish card"*. His greatest objective was to break Britain's power to wage war in Europe by forcing the withdrawal of her troops and disrupting the commerce that created the wealth that subsidised Britain's allies in Europe.

Among the Jacobite conspirators paving the way for the French descent upon Scotland were several Fife lairds, including Malcolm of Grange and Balfour of Bethune, both of whom had East Neuk estates. In the event the first - and probably the most promising - attempt to restore the Stuart dynasty had brought James into the Firth of Forth with a powerful fleet of 28 French ships, including 5 line-of-battle ships and over 20 fast well-gunned frigates. Malcolm of Grange had been primed to provide pilots to guide the ships up the Forth, and to arrange for local fishing boats and other small craft to land the troops.

The expedition was on a scale well equal to its task, which was to take control of Scotland and provide security for the Jacobites while they mustered their Scottish army, planned to number about 30,000 men or more. There were 5000 French troops in the invasion fleet. There were only 2000 garrison troops in Edinburgh, not of front-line quality. The best regiments were with Marlborough on the continent.

However things had gone badly wrong for the French fleet and the threatened landing never took place. Malcolm had played his part effectively, but to no purpose. The French had come from Dunkirk, where strong winds and mists had enabled the ships to elude a strong blockading fleet under Admiral Byng. Sailing out of sight of land to escape detection, they had so far overshot their destination as to make their landfall on the coast of Aberdeenshire. It was after re-tracing many wasted sea-miles that they anchored near the May on the evening of 12 March. Meantime, on the morning of 12 March, a delayed French frigate *Le Protée*, commanded by Lieutenant de Frégat Rambures, had been able to enter the Forth off Dunbar, where she was met by Malcolm with a fleet of small craft. Rambures sailed up the Firth, meeting more and more small craft and assurances of support. Meantime the French naval commander, Admiral Forbin, with the main fleet was coming down the coast of Angus; and Admiral Byng in pursuit was somewhere near Berwick. By midnight Byng was able to bring his fleet to anchor some miles to the east of the May. Forbin had anchored between the May and the East Neuk.

It was a close-run thing; but Forbin saw his enemy in the morning and knew that his 28 ships were not a match for Byng who had 26 line-of-battle ships as well as frigates. By skilful manoeuvring Forbin was able to elude Byng once again, and the greater speed of his vessels brought them clear away, escaping to the north with the loss of a single ship. For a time James hoped that a landing might be made in Aberdeenshire or in the Moray Firth but Forbin insisted on withdrawing altogether and the expedition came to nothing.

Not the least extraordinary thing about the whole episode is that, despite the arrest of about 20 Jacobite peers and a slightly greater number of other gentlemen, no Scots Jacobite was brought to justice in Scotland. Clever politicking in London by the Duke of Hamilton, who had played an equivocal part in the plotting, and the useful Scots verdict of not proven, had saved all those arrested, to the indignation of the Parliament in Westminster. Malcolm of Grange seems to have been able to conceal his part in the affair. One factor inhibiting the pressing of prosecutions in Scotland was that too many Scots in high places might have been implicated.

The next attempt to put James on the throne had much more serious effects in Fife. In 1715 Elie Harbour was involved in the opening stages of the rising of that year, when the Earl of Mar landed there early in August on his way to start the rebellion at Braemar. Under Queen Anne, Mar had been Secretary of State for Scotland,

but he was dismissed from office in 1714 by Queen Anne's successor, the Hanoverian George I. At the beginning of August Mar left London surreptitiously by sea, and sailed via Newcastle to Elie. He immediately went to Balfour of Bethune's house at Kilrenny, where he met some Fife Jacobite lairds including Malcolm of Grange. Mar was able to cross into Angus on 17 August with an escort of forty Fife horsemen, on his way to Braemar for the great gathering called for 17 August, where he launched the rebellion. The speed with which these events took place is evidence of much preliminary planning.

There was little or no resistance to the insurgents north of the Forth, and for a considerable time the whole of the east coast from the Forth to the Moray Firth was dominated by the Jacobites. The Royal Navy had cruisers off the coast and controlled the waters of the Forth estuary but ships from France that eluded the cruisers could land supplies at almost any port further north. Until December of 1715 there were no government troops in Fife to resist the insurgents.

During this period Sir John Anstruther, who was no Jacobite, lay low. When a Jacobite party raided Elie House looking for weapons and valuables to raise funds for the cause, Sir John was not there, and his treasures were well concealed. Wood says that Mackintosh, Sir John's groom, was pressed to reveal the hiding place and that on his refusing he was nailed by his ear to a large tree "*for an obstinate Whig*".

The Forth was well-guarded in its upper reaches and was a major obstacle to Mar in his attempts to march south. In October, he sent a force of 2500 men under MacIntosh of Borlum into the East Neuk to cross into East Lothian. On the night of 12 October about 1600 men successfully crossed in boats commandeered from harbours from Crail to Earlsferry. A second fleet was intercepted by the Royal Navy on the following night, but most of the rebel troops were able to escape back to the Fife coast. The inhabitants of the East Neuk burghs would not enjoy these visitations. Malcolm had played some part in arranging the crossings; but in a letter which seems to be making a comment on a report from Malcolm that some of the detachments had crossed from Earlsferry Mar commented "*that fool Malcolm is capable of nothing but lying*". None the less, it seems certain that the fishermen of Earlsferry would have been pressed into service to enable the Jacobite forces to take advantage of the shortest crossing.

MacIntosh's party was foiled in Edinburgh, but formed the nucleus of a small Jacobite army that entered the north of England and was joined by a considerable number of English Jacobites. The force was ultimately completely surrounded by larger Government forces and obliged to surrender at Preston on 14 November.

The insurgents dominated Fife until after the battle of Sheriffmuir near Dunblane on 13 November, raising funds and collecting arms wherever they could. At Sheriffmuir Government forces under the Duke of Argyle fought a drawn battle against much superior numbers, which left Argyle in possession of the field and frustrated Mar's intention to march to the south. The engagements at Preston and Sheriffmuir effectively ended Mar's hopes.

Before the end of December Argyle's little army had been re-inforced by Dutch troops, and with the Royal Navy in command of the Forth it was easy to send detachments to clear the insurgents from the Fife harbours. This effectively ended the disturbances in Fife, although Mar's forces remained in control of Perth and the area around it until the end of January. The Old Pretender had landed at Peterhead, and joined Mar at Perth on 6 January; but his presence had become irrelevant, and on 3 February he boarded a ship at Montrose and returned to France.

Some retributive action followed for the Fife lairds and others who had joined Mar; but in Scotland it was difficult if not impossible to secure convictions in the courts and only a few Scots were put to death under martial law. It was far otherwise in England where many of those taken in arms were executed in Lancashire and London. MacIntosh successfully escaped from Newgate, and lived to return to Scotland "*to be a benefactor of his country by promoting its agriculture*", which he did by his writings about agricultural improvement while a prisoner in Edinburgh Castle. A general indemnity in 1716 covered almost all those who had taken part in the rising; but Balfour of Bethune had to emigrate from Scotland to France and his estates passed after his death to his sister Ann: when estates were forfeited for treason it was usually only for the life of the offender. Malcolm's estates also passed

to another branch of the family.

In 1745 there was little support for the Stuart cause in Fife, despite the early success of the Jacobites at Prestonpans in September. After the middle of September when Prince Charles ("*the Young Pretender*") took control of Edinburgh, apart from the Castle which remained in Government hands, no doubt the ferries across the Forth carried some of the curious to see the Prince and the interesting scene around him. The ferry service had been interrupted, but a letter of November 6 reported that "the Kinghorn Ferry is now open". There was still a Malcolm at Grange, but no indication that he took any part in the rising. The most prominent East Neuk supporter of Prince Charles was the Earl of Kellie, who attempted to raise a regiment on his behalf. According to the 19th century account of the rebellion by Robert Chambers, the regiment consisted of Kellie as the colonel, another elderly Fife laird as the lieutenant-colonel, and a single serving-man to represent all the other ranks. In a letter of 30 October the sister of Lady Logie Almond reported that Lord Kellie wanted to march south with the Prince, but "*they were so wise as to give him some post in Fife to keep him behind and well will he execute his Office*". After the rebellion the Earl was confined in Edinburgh Castle for three years, but he escaped prosecution because he was considered to be feeble-minded.

After Prestonpans the Jacobites were sufficiently in control of Fife to send captured government officers on parole to stay in Culross, Cupar, Leslie and St. Andrews. Charles was always in need of money and officers acting for him levied a property tax called the "cess" from burghs and landed proprietors wherever they could. The Earl of Cromarty, based in Perth, was the head tax collector for Fife, and no doubt East Neuk lairds and burghs were visited.

HARBOUR FINANCES AND TRADE IN 1740

The Jacobite incursions in the first half of the century, though alarming and damaging and very detrimental to the lives and interests of a few, did not greatly alter the underlying pattern of social and economic change. In the East Neuk the Anstruthers of Elie continued the expansion and development of their extensive estates. In 1740 Sir John decided to set out the harbour and other dues which he was entitled to charge in a formal legal document which was headed "Roll of the Customs, Shore Dues & Anchorages of Elie".

Appendix I. is a transcript. The "*toun customs*" were charges which Sir John as the baron of the baronial burgh was entitled to levy on trade carried on in his burgh and certain goods crossing the burgh boundary. The shore dues were charges made on goods landed at or shipped from the shore, which means the quay at Elie Harbour. The anchorage dues were what would now be called mooring or berthing dues. Some of the "*toun customs*" were still being exacted in the 19th century. The terms of the ordinance with which the document ends shows that Sir John was acting not only as the owner of the harbour but also as a feudal baron exercising his heritable jurisdiction over his barony. The power to confiscate and sell goods depended on that, and not on his ownership of the harbour.

> "*I Doe Ordain the Customs & Duties contained on the Seven Foregoing pages to be regularly Exacted by the Tacksmen or Commissioners thereof, And in case of Failure, to poind, Arrest or distress by Sale of Goods For payment of the Same; & for so doing this to one & every of them Shall be their Warrant Given under my hand & Seal Att Elie house the fifteenth Day of October Seventeen Hundred and Fourtie in presence of James Elder And Benjamin Plenderleath both my Servants*
> (signed) J. Anstruther
> (Signed) James Elder witness
> (signed) David Plenderleath witness
> 15 October 1740*"

The Tacksmen referred to were persons who were prepared to offer an annual sum (the "*tack*") for the right to collect and keep the dues. Under an alternative arrangement the owner of the harbour might choose to appoint Commissioners whom he would pay to collect the dues on his behalf.

The shore dues listed in the Roll were apparently at the same rate for goods being shipped or goods being landed, though here and there are one or two entries which indicate in which direction the goods were going. Strangers are usually required to pay higher rates than inhabitants of the burgh. It is evident from the entry under Toun Customs relating to grain put into the granary but not shipped that in 1740 there was an export trade in grain. There

is evidence from later years of grain and potatoes being shipped to the Continent; and in accordance with relative scarcity in different countries the grain trade across the North Sea could flow either way. One charge listed specifically mentions herrings as a coastways export.

There is a reflection of Sabbath observance in the two entries referring to "*Salt great or small*". Small salt was the regular daily product of the saltpans: the salters collected great salt from the pans only on Monday. No salt was made on the Sabbath, though sufficient fire was maintained (a work of necessity) to prevent the pans from cooling too much. This allowed the salt to crystallize more slowly than usual, producing the large crystals of great salt. The harbour dues for the two classes were the same.

Ironstone quarried or mined locally was for shipping to ironworks elsewhere, which in 1740 probably meant the Carron iron works near Falkirk. In the 19th century ironstone mined from the Earlsferry links area was for a time a very important export, much of it going to the Newcastle area. Smiddie coal, charged at a lower rate than other coal, presumably was low quality coal and an export item. Much of the list clearly prescribes dues on imported goods, e.g. "*Wine or Brandie p Tun*". The named goods on the Roll include only goods produced in the Elie area, or goods used in the area. It does not include some of the many goods in common use at that period and found in customs records for other ports, which suggests that the Roll records the type of goods that were actually being landed at and shipped from Elie in 1740. It does not read like a copy of some standard list or of the list of dues for a port like Leith, Kirkcaldy or Dundee, where a much larger range of goods would have been listed.

The shore dues on timber, charged at one piece for every hundred, were the same as those authorised in William Scott's Royal Charter of 1601; but in 1740 the dues on other goods were specified in much greater detail. In 1601 all other cargoes were simply charged at one standard rate per ton, except for the rate for merchant goods ready for sale which was 50% higher. The variety of dues set out in 1740 would require much more inspection of cargoes by the collectors.

There were special dues called "*teinds*", common to most if not all privately-owned fishing ports, requiring the payment of every tenth fish for fish caught by Elie fishers, brought into Elie harbour or sold by them to other boats at sea. The other boats at sea might be Dutch herring "busses" or boats from Fisherrow buying additional fish to sell in Edinburgh. If Elie fishers themselves transported their catches to other harbours they had to pay half teinds in Elie. Stranger boats landing fish at Elie also paid half teinds. With the same rules in place at other harbours no catch in theory at least could escape paying the full teind, but evasion would not be very difficult.

The dues on vessels using the harbour are set out in a page headed "Anchorage Duties". These charges, which had been two shillings (Scots) per ton of capacity in 1601, were in 1740 for British vessels one penny sterling per "*Nett tun*". This would seem to be about half the earlier rate, though the rules for measuring tonnage had changed a bit, to give rather higher figures in the latter year. The rates were halved for boats belonging to Elie. There were higher rates for foreign vessels, and much higher rates for "*passage boats*" to Kinghorn or other ferry ports. This suggests that a common way of travelling to Edinburgh was to take a boat along the Fife coast to one of the ferry ports serving Leith. Drave boats (fishing boats following the herring shoals) paid even higher dues, as did "*Couper Boats*", the boats which served the herring curers by carrying their barrels, salt and other equipment as well as transporting the finished products. Other fishing boats were charged according to size.

The page on anchorage dues ends with a signed statement by the man who originally wrote out the document for Sir John, Robert Maltman. He declares that the dues recorded were the anchorage dues fixed by "the Late Deceased Old Sir John Anstruther Baronet". This note must have been added to the document after Sir John died in 1753, at the age of 77. Perhaps some dispute had arisen about the validity of the charges being made.

Below Maltman's statement, and therefore perhaps a later addition to the list of dues, is an entry recording a charge called "*Dockmaill*" for every vessel built at Elie. For inhabitants this was five shillings and for strangers ten. It would presumably have been payable when the vessel was first "*docked*", i.e. launched into the harbour.

The next section of the Roll sets out the "Rules to be observed by all Masters of Vessells that comes to the Elie harbour". These rules are backed by the heavy "Penalty of Five Pounds Sterling for Disobeying the Shoarmasters Orders".

The final section, before Sir John's concluding ordinance giving legal force to the Roll, details the "Toun Customs". These included charges for weighing goods, which means Sir John had a tron, or weighing machine, which might have been placed where it could serve the harbour also, possibly somewhere near the Toll Green; charges on meal and malt sold in the town, on some foodstuffs and other goods brought into the toun; on timber and millstones carried from the toun; and on stranger hawkers selling cloth, ribbons and hardware. There were charges for grain brought into the toun and put into the granary; and if the stored grain was not shipped but sold in the toun an additional charge had to be paid. Most of the charges were at higher rates for strangers than for inhabitants. These customs were separate from and apparently additional to the shore dues that would have been charged on goods that had been landed at the harbour, e.g. timber and millstones.

The mention of a granary is interesting. It shows that by 1740 there was a sufficient grain surplus produced in the area for it to be worthwhile to build a granary to receive and store it, building up quantities worth shipping to Edinburgh, England or overseas, according to demand. There is no evidence of the existence of an earlier granary building in the main part of Elie; and the reference to shipping the stored grain is in such terms as to imply that local sale of the stored grain was the exception. This suggests that the granary would be at the harbour, where the most likely site on the Law would be the one on which the surviving granary building was erected later in the century.

The 1740 roll of dues gives us the fullest picture we are likely to have of the kind of trade carried on at Elie Harbour in the 18th century, but of course it does not show the quantities of goods passing through the harbour. After 1748 it would no longer be possible for the Baron of Elie to exercise the same authority to lay down the law for his barony as is shown in the words in the ordinance decreeing the way in which his harbour dues were to be enforced by the confiscation and sale of goods if necessary. Parliament passed in that year a much needed Act which effectively abolished the hereditary local jurisdictions of Scotland. These had been the source of many abuses and acts of oppression. After the passing of the Act, baronial courts were restricted to relatively trifling matters. Burton says that the sums paid in compensation to those whose judicial rights were extinguished, though not very large (about £150,000 for the whole of Scotland), gave landed proprietors significant additional means to finance the improvements in agriculture that were growing in importance at that time.

7
Shipping growth and harbour decay

1759 – ROUP OF THE HARBOUR DUES – THE SEA BOX

Some dim light on activity at the harbour around the middle of the century is shed by the records of what happened in 1759, the famous Annus Mirabilis of British victories over the French in the Seven Years War. In that year the Tack for two years of the Shore Dues, Anchorages, Teind Fish, and Customs of Elie was put up for sale by roup, on 22 August at an upset price of £15 sterling a year. The document setting forth the formal Articles of Roup ends with the following added note "*N.B. No person offering after it was sett up at £15 sterling the roup was adjourned*". An appended agreement signed by "*David Chalmers vintner in Elie and James Wood Mercht. there*" records that they took the Tack at £14 a year. The articles impose harbour master duties on the Tacksman, including the duty not to permit digging for worms or bait within the harbour, a prohibition still contained in the modern Harbour Bye-laws. The Tacksman was also required to "*take care that no Ballast or Rubish be cast in the Harbour, & shall notice the reight mooring of the vessels from time to time, and shall be liable for his neglect in that, and shall furnish plank for the use of the Shore on his owen charge*". The "*plank*" to be furnished would no doubt be planks for use as gangplanks between ships and the quay, an essential piece of equipment at a harbour receiving ships alongside.

In addition to the right to collect the dues specified in the Roll the articles provide that "*the Tacksmen shall be obliged to collect the Ringage or Ringmoney from the respective vessels at one pennie Scots per ton and shall quarterly pay the profits thereof to the factor of the Sea box of Elie, and shall have one Shilling and Six pennies Scots for Each pound Scots money collected and that for the Trouble of collecting the Same*". The term Ringage or Ringmoney seems to mean a charge for a vessel berthed against the pier or the shore (the quay) and tying up to metal rings there. At one penny Scots per ton the charge added less than 10%

to even the lowest anchorage dues.

The payment to the Sea Box of Elie raises the interesting possibility that, despairing of the laird ever investing any money in even the smallest improvement at the harbour, the skippers of Elie had instead invested some of the funds of their Sea Box to provide mooring rings. This is the kind of practical improvement, not too costly, that would appeal to the skippers who financed and controlled the Sea Box Society and benefited from it in their retirement years; and the charge would no doubt have been set at a level that brought the Sea Box a worthwhile return. The Society's Royal Charter is dated 1830, when it was granted by William IV. It also bears the signature of the Home Secretary, Robert Peel, who led the House of Commons under the Premiership of the Duke of Wellington. The opening words of the Charter clearly show that it was being granted to an already well established society.

A FISHING TRAGEDY

In a footnote to the Statistical Account of the parish published in 1793 we catch a glimpse of a tragedy for the fishing community of Earlsferry in 1766. The account records that seven of the eighteen fishermen of the burgh drowned in the sinking of a single boat. This must have been one of the larger boats in use in the area at that time. In later years fishing from Earlsferry was carried on in small boats suitable only for in-shore fishing, and the burgh did not benefit from the great 19th century development of the white fish and particularly herring fisheries that brought prosperity to the small fishing towns of eastern Scotland. The writer says that there had been only a few employed in fishing; but from what is said elsewhere in the account it is clear that fishing remained an important activity there.

JAMES HORSBURGH

In the period around 1770 Elie harbour would see much of a boy who was to become by far Elie's most famous seaman. James Horsburgh, born in 1762, was the son of parents so poor that his school education alternated with periods of farm labour. However, Elie was a place that fostered seamen, and James learned mathematics, navigation, and book-keeping at the local school before going to sea at 16. A boy with his interests would have spent much of his spare time among the boats and ships at the harbour, and when he left school he would easily find employment in a locally-owned ship. His early years as a ship's boy, the first rung on the ladder, were spent in the coal trade, shipping coal to Holland and to other continental ports like Ostend and Hamburg.

James rose in the merchant service, and became an expert navigator. He was inspired to take up the making of charts by being wrecked because of defective charts on the island of Diego Garcia while sailing from Batavia to Ceylon as first mate of the Atlas. He became a master chart maker, drawing and etching highly accurate charts from his own observations. He was able to compile and publish a major piece of work which became the standard sailing directions for the seas between the Cape of Good Hope, India, China, the East Indies and Australia, known to him as New Holland. He made several important discoveries in oceanography and meteorology, and his scientific achievements led to his election as a Fellow of the Royal Society in 1806. In 1810 he was appointed hydrographer to the wealthy and powerful East India Company. From 1810 until 1836, the year in which he died, he continued to chart the eastern seas, and published works on meteorology at sea and marine surveying. He is commemorated in Elie by a plaque on the house in Bank Street in which he was born.

JOHN PAUL JONES IN THE FORTH
In 1779 an unwelcome visitor appeared off the East Neuk shore, initially received with great courtesy by Sir John Anstruther. One of the founders of the US Navy, John Paul Jones, raiding round the coasts of Britain with a small squadron led by his powerful ship, the *Bonhomme Richard*, anchored off Pittenweem. Mistaking the ships for friendly vessels expected at that time to be returning from Africa, Sir John sent off one of his own boats, in which were two Elie skippers, John Ovenstone and James Adamson, with a gift of fresh fruit and vegetables and some newspapers. He thought these

gifts would be very welcome to the sailors returning from a long voyage. Wood quotes a song composed about the incident in which Jones's response is recorded.

"Sir John sent to see
What ships they might be,
With a basket of fruit, and the news, man.
They sent back the boat
With powder and shot,
And bade him defend Elie House, man"

It is clear how the word "*house*" is to be pronounced. The Elie skippers, it appears, returned safely with Sir John's boat. A Pittenweem pilot, Andrew Paton, was not so fortunate. Jones kept him on board to make use of his expertise, and released him some time later in a Dutch port when his services were no longer required. Wood says he received "*a handsome remuneration*".

Burton reports that around this time there was concern in the Firth of Forth ports about enemy incursions, and some enthusiasm among seamen in the area to join the Navy and serve against the enemy. At the same time a combined Spanish and French fleet supporting the Americans in their War of Independence was dominating the English Channel. The enthusiasm of the sailors of the Forth became of little significance, because the Government's response to the naval threat was to re-introduce impressment, not used since the naval struggle against the Dutch in the 1660s. This made possible a great increase in strength for the Royal Navy, since the law said any able-bodied seaman was liable to be impressed. This would present many problems for the seafaring community of Elie.

THE STATISTICAL ACCOUNT OF SCOTLAND
Some information about harbour activities in Elie and Earlsferry is to be found in the accounts of the parishes of Elie and Kilconquhar (to which Earlsferry then belonged) given by the parish ministers to Sir John Sinclair for his ground-breaking *Statistical Account of Scotland* in the 1790s.

The Reverend Alexander Small of Kilconquhar recorded in his contribution, published in 1793, that Earlsferry had a population of about 350, out of 2013 in the whole parish. He reports that "*there is one sloop and a few small fishing boats, belonging to Earlsferry*". There were 21 sailors in the parish, a proportion of whom would perhaps be fishermen, a category he does not distinguish separately. Most if not all of the 21 sailors in Kilconquhar parish would have lived in Earlsferry. Curiously, though coal-mining continued in Earlsferry into the second half of the 19th century, he does not list miners or colliers in the section where he records numbers in various occupations; but elsewhere he describes extensive coalfields and records numbers of employees at several pits, totalling over 100. He does not record any coal-mining at this time near Earlsferry but plenty elsewhere in the parish.

Mr. Small reports that great quantities of fish are caught and sold locally, and fish are sent to the Edinburgh market. Cod, skate, ling, turbot, and various kinds of shell-fish are to be found "*in great plenty on the coast in all seasons*", but "*haddocks, for which our coast is famous, have deserted us for some years past*". Sea-ware from the coast was collected by farmers and made excellent manure for barley.

The reference to a "*sloop*" suggests that at that time there was still one vessel engaged in the cargo trade based at the harbour. From the "TABLE OF CUSTOMS SHORE DUES AND ANCHORAGES" approved by the Council in 1804 it appears there was no cargo trade at the harbour by that date. The only shore dues listed are a charge of 2 pence for each open boat for one year, and of a halfpenny for each hundred fishes sold by fishermen in the town.

In his account of Elie (which he spells "Ely") published in 1796 the Rev. William Pairman records the population of the parish as 620. He does not list the numbers in different occupations, but reports as follows on fisheries: - "*There are 8 fishermen belonging to this parish. They have houses, rent free, from Sir John Anstruther, superior of this place, on condition of their supplying the town of Ely with fish at least three times a week. They are well situated for carrying on the fisheries, and, on the whole, are pretty successful*". We know, of course, that even if the fishermen lived rent free they paid Sir John Anstruther "*teind*" fish, one in every ten of the fish they landed.

The account records that the coal supply for the parish, not surprisingly, comes from "*an excellent coalwork, belonging to Sir John Anstruther, 3 miles from this parish*". Coal prices, per cart load of 75 stones bought at the mine, were 2s. 6d. or less in

Kilconquhar, and 4s to 5s according to quality, from Sir John's pit at Pittenweem. There would be no competing coal sellers in Elie; but Sir John's coal was widely recognised to be of very high quality and was in much demand at Pittenweem harbour for export to the continent.

CONDITION OF THE HARBOUR

Mr. Pairman's description of the harbour shows that at the end of the 18th century, as at the end of the 17th the harbour was in need of major repairs:

"*There is an excellent harbour at Ely. It is the deepest in the Frith of Forth, Bruntisland excepted. It has remarkably easy access, and is perfectly safe. It is the resort of more wind-bound vessels, than any other harbour, perhaps, in Scotland. It has also been the means of saving many a ship, cargo, and seaman, that would otherwise have been driven out of the Frith; many of them being so poorly manned and provisioned, that they would never have been able to regain the coast. This useful harbour, however, is going fast to ruin. It is much to be wished, that some public spirited person would recommend it to the attention of the Chamber of Commerce, or the Convention of Royal Burghs, to obtain some aid to put it into a better state. An inconsiderable expence, in proportion to the importance and utility of the object, would completely repair it. It may be remarked, also, that the value of the shipping brought in, bears but a small proportion to that of their cargoes, which are often grain and other perishable commodities, that might suffer by being exposed to a storm, even though the ship were to weather it.*"

Mr. Pairman also records that "*There are, belonging to this place, seven square-rigged vessels, carrying 1000 or 1100 tons, all employed in foreign trade, and one sloop used as a coaster. Vessels, of considerable size, are built here*". These sizeable ships, averaging about 150 tons in carrying capacity, belonged to Elie shipowners, and would almost certainly have been manned by Elie crews and maintained and possibly built in Elie, but most if not all of their shipments on which valuable dues had to be paid would be landed in larger ports like Leith, Boness, Kirkcaldy and Dundee.

Mr. Pairman does not suggest that the owner of the harbour might do something about the state of the harbour. In the section of the account which lists the local landowners we may see why he had to be careful: "*Proprietors & c. Sir John Anstruther is patron of the church and sole proprietor of the parish, one single farm excepted ....*"

At first sight it appears surprising that with a small merchant fleet using Elie as a base, and an active shipyard, the wealthy proprietor did not keep his harbour in proper repair. This suggests that the 17th century pattern continued. Elie ships brought little traffic or revenue to their home port. Though Elie was valuable as a harbour of refuge this was not a use that brought in any significant revenue. It seems clear successive Anstruther lairds saw no similar advantage to investing in Elie Harbour.

Though the harbour belonged to Sir John the coal and salt his mines and saltpans produced were exported from the pier which Anstruther money had built in Pittenweem Harbour for this purpose. Salt and coal were transported to the pier by the horse-drawn railway which ran from his

St. Philips saltpans near St. Monans. There were, however, several collieries near Elie, including the Grange Colliery on Earlsferry Links, for which Elie Harbour was a convenient place to ship coal, though Earlsferry harbour was nearer. It is interesting, in view of all the coal produced locally, that the Elie House Accounts for 1813 show two shipments of 32 tons each of Wemyss coal, shipped from the Wemyss estates harbour of Methil, being unloaded at "*Ely Shoar*" the harbour quay and carted from there to Elie House. It is possible that there were problems at that time with the seams at the Anstruthers' collieries that produced the best house coal. It is certain that the Wemyss coal-mines, working productive seams and with horse-drawn railways to the estate's export harbour at Methil, could deliver coal on the Forth at the most competitive prices.

8

Decades of neglect

The nineteenth century was to see the greatest improvements to the harbour since 1600 and with the coming of the steamship a great increase in traffic both in cargo and in passengers. By the end of the century, however, the size of the seafaring community in Elie had greatly diminished, and the ships that carried most of the traffic were owned and based elsewhere. An important early development was the building of a new granary; but after that there were several decades during which the fabric of the harbour was allowed to deteriorate badly. It was not until the middle of the century that large investments by a new owner rescued and greatly extended its structures to form the substantial harbour we see today, which would have been very much larger if the Admiralty had not effectively vetoed his most ambitious plans.

THE NEW GRANARY

The parish ministers' accounts of Elie and Kilconquhar, written in the 1790s, both tell of the far-reaching changes and the increased rents that the improved farms brought to the estate owners. It was very much in the interests of any landed proprietor to improve the means of getting the produce of his estates to the market. The Kilconquhar account is explicit about the importance of the export trade. Oats and oat-meal sometimes had to be imported into the parish, because the best land was devoted to more valuable crops. Mr. Small says "*we export considerable quantities of wheat, barley, pease and beans, and some potatoes*". The natural outlet for Kilconquhar and other nearby parishes as well as Elie would be the harbour of Elie, if adequate facilities for handling exports were available there.

It is therefore not surprising that the only development that took place around this time took the form of a new granary at the harbour (2), which must have replaced the one referred to in Sir John's Ordinance of 1740. A larger building would be needed to handle the greatly increased production of the area. Title to the granary was granted by Sir John's son and heir, Sir Philip Anstruther, by way

of feu to his younger brother Robert, Colonel of the Tay Fencibles, in 1808. The deed grants the Colonel a plot 76 feet by 36 feet "*whereon a Granary is lately built by the said Colonel Robert Anstruther*". The grant conveys to Robert only the bare solum on which the granary had been erected, but also includes appropriate access rights, including the right to form a cart road round the granary. There is provision for a "*Covered Outshot*" on the north gable, which permits the construction of a "*Spout of ten feet long , by eleven feet broad....for loading vessels within the said harbour of Elie*". The "spout", as shown in the photograph (2), was still in use until well into the 20th century.

There is clear evidence that, despite the great progress of agriculture made in the 18th century, it was not until after the turn of the century that the old granary was replaced. This comes from tree-ring dating of the timbers removed from the granary when it was recently gutted for conversion into flats. An article in the Tayside Fife Archaeological Journal for 2002 (No. 8) reports that though the larger timbers removed from the building are not yet dateable, small oak timbers forming key parts of the massive post-and-beam structure that supported the floors can be identified as coming from trees felled in North Germany between 1802 and 1818. With the date in Colonel Robert's title this narrows the period of construction to 1802-1808.

There appears to be no record or relic to show the location of the earlier granary; but there is an implication in the language of the 1740 Ordinance that its primary purpose was to store grain for shipping. This would suggest it might have been on the site on which the new granary was built. With careful management of the building programme, and taking advantage of the partly seasonal nature of the trade, it might have been possible to demolish the old granary and build anew without serious interference to shipments.

The annual Feu-duty for the granary was set at only one shilling and eightpence; but the deed also provided that the superior could charge the feuar with the payment of a proportion, to be determined by the superior, of the salary paid to *"the Schoolmaster of Elie present and to come"*. The amount (whether this was of the whole salary or the proportion is not clear) was not to exceed *"one hundred pounds money"*. The feuar would have little fear that the figure would be reached at an early date. In the 1790s the schoolmaster's salary was £11 a year, to which he could add some fees. By about 1855 it had risen to £34 4s plus fees on top.

THE COAST GUARD STATION

The Coastguard Service (HM Coastguard in later usage) was established by a Treasury Minute of 1822. It took over duties that had been performed by several separate services, mainly concerned with the suppression of smuggling. It was part of the establishment of the Board of Customs, but its officers were nominated by the Admiralty, and held naval rank. In 1856 the service was transferred to the Admiralty, and was manned almost entirely by naval ratings under naval officers, the whole complement becoming a naval reserve. In 1925 it was taken over by the Board of Trade.

Elie was never important enough as a port to require a custom-house; but in the New Statistical Account of Anstruther Easter published in 1837 it is recorded that a custom-house had been established there in 1827, presumably as part of the re-organisation of services begun in 1822, with Elie as one of its subordinate ports where a coast-waiter was employed. This was a responsible post with the function of ensuring that no dutiable imports by-passed the customs officers. The signature of *"Jas. Adamson"* with the designation *"coast-waiter"* appears on the petition of 1834 pressing the proprietor to repair the harbour.

By 1839 there were 33 coastguard stations in Scotland, of which Elie was one, the base for Lieutenant Randall, recorded in the 1830s as Commanding the Coastguard in Fife. At Elie itself there were at least five other coastguards. Later in the century the handsome stone buildings of the Coastguard Station, reached from the Toft by Admiralty Lane, provided both homes and workplace for the Coastguards. There was a look-out post on the summit of Shepherd Law just inland from Elie Ness, with a commanding view of the Firth and a nearby mast for practical rescue exercises. When later in the century the station was

supplied with breeches buoy apparatus for rescue operations a track was formed from the station to the east end of the Toft beside Braehead Cottage to allow the breeches buoy carriage quick access to the shore road.

Over time the service developed both in its function as a naval reserve, with training in small arms and at sea, as well as its coast-watch and anti-smuggling duties, and rescue from ships in distress on the coast.

Lieutenant (later Captain) Randall took an active interest in Elie Harbour, and was one of those who signed a petition to the proprietor in the 1830s asking him to put the harbour in proper repair. He supplied invaluable help to William Bald, the Admiralty's Commissioner who wrote a critical report on the state of the harbour in 1848, including his own calculation of the true amount of the harbour's annual income at that period. Members of the Coastguard Service were active in the community in a variety of ways.

CONDITION OF THE HARBOUR BEFORE 1850

At the beginning of the century the pier had deteriorated so far that a notice was issued to mariners in July 1808 stating the point of the pier was down and that a quantity of displaced stones was lying round it. Shipmasters were warned to keep some distance from where the point had been. Contractors were invited to tender for the work of re-building the point of the pier, but nothing came of this. Plans (5) for large scale improvements of the harbour prepared for the proprietor in 1815 by the engineer Robert Stevenson, show that by that date about 40 feet of the outer end of the pier had been swept away and a further 30 feet or so was badly broken down. This left about 100 feet of usable pier, and a slightly longer length of the old quay dating from 1600 where ships could berth alongside to load and unload cargoes. The scene depicted on the cover is from an oil painting of 1848 by Charles Blyth; and it shows a ship nosing into the old quay.

The Elie estate accounts for 1813 record that the swarf dyke was repaired in that year, when Thomas Finlay was paid £56 18s 6p for *"building the sea dyke at Elie Shoar"*. The Stevenson plan of 1815 shows the dyke and the roadway beside it as if they were in reasonable shape. At that date the high sea walls protecting the sea gardens and the roadway

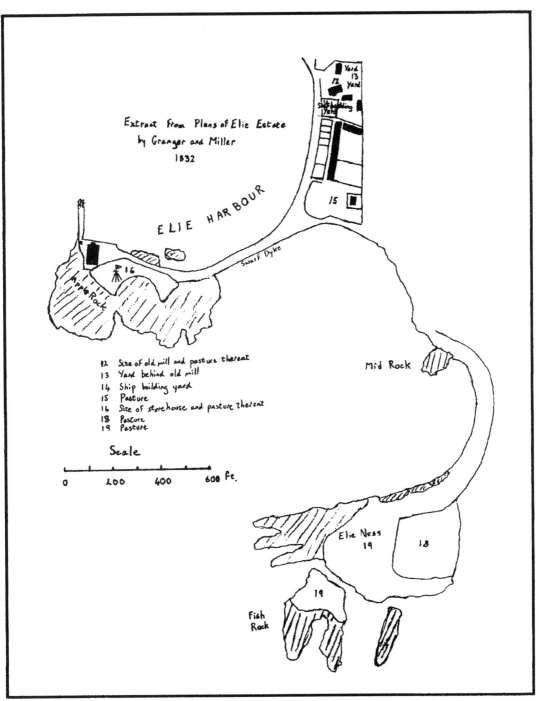

Extract from Plans of Elie Estate
by Granger and Miller
1832

ELIE HARBOUR

Yard 13 Yard

12

Shipbuilding Yard

15

Swarf Dyke

Apple Rock

P 16

Mid Rock

12 Site of old mill and pasture thereat
13 Yard behind old mill
14 Ship building yard
15 Pasture
16 Site of storehouse and pasture thereat
18 Pasture
19 Pasture

Scale

0   200   400   600 ft.

Elie Ness
19

18

Fish Rock

19

10. Estate plan of harbour area - 1832

STEAM
TO
EDINBURGH, GLASGOW, & the SOUTH.

 The Edinburgh and Dundee Steam-Packet Company's New Steam-Ship
"BRITANNIA,"
SAILS REGULARLY
FROM DUNDEE FOR GRANTON PIER
Every afternoon at Two o'clock;
AND FROM GRANTON PIER
Every morning at Eight o'clock;—
Making the Passage in Four Hours—.
CALLING AT ELIE, ANSTRUTHER, AND CRAIL.
FARES:—
Cabin, 4s.; Steerage, 2s. 6d.

*** Parties from Edinburgh, returning same day, one Fare only; and Pleasure Parties on Saturdays, from Dundee. returning on Mondays, one Fare only.

This fine new iron Steamer BRITANNIA, of 207 Tons Register and 150 Horse Power, of a beautiful model by Mr W. Denny, is fitted up in a commodious style, with separate State Rooms for parties or families, water-tight Bulkheads, Life-Boats on deck, and other improvements; and will materially abridge the time hitherto taken on this passage.

Mr Croall's Coaches leave the Duty-House, Edinburgh, and Mr Coulston's Coach leaves his Office, Leith, at half-past Seven morning, and wait the vessel's arrival.

FROM EDINBURGH—The BRITANNIA will arrive in time for the Evening Train to Glasgow at half-past Seven.

FROM GRANTON—Steamer to Berwick and Newcastle every Tuesday. Wednesday, and Friday morning at Seven o'clock, and every Saturday afternoon at Six o'clock—FARES, 10s. and 6s.

FROM LEITH—Steamer to Hull every Wednesday and Saturday, about High Water—FARES, 12s. and 7s. 6d.

JOHN BELL, AGENT.

Dundee, September 1845,

11. 1845 Steamship service

along the Toft had not been built and the road at this point simply ran along the shore just above high water. The Stevenson plan does not show the sea gardens of the Toft.

On his own initiative Stevenson had included in his plan two breakwaters to enclose Wood Haven (which he called Wade's Bay) to provide a harbour in which ships would remain afloat except at the lowest tides. He also sketched a long mole extending towards the pier in a south-easterly direction from the foot of what is now Rankeillor Street to give the harbour a large area of sheltered water, though all of it would continue to dry out at low tide. These plans were prepared for the Sir John Anstruther, nephew of Sir Philip, who had succeeded to the estate in 1811; but when he died in 1818 he had taken no steps to carry them out.

Estate plans prepared in 1832 (10) seem to show that some repair work might have been done near the outer end of the pier; but these plans were not prepared by an engineer and may not accurately represent the condition of the pier. The surveyors were mainly concerned to delineate the properties on the estate clearly, and they do show the Toft sea gardens. The detailed report by William Bald prepared about 1848 states categorically that after 1808 no work was done on the pier for thirty-two years. It was not until 1842 that substantial repairs were carried out.

At the beginning of the century it appears the Swarf Dyke had been in reasonably good condition. It had clearly fallen into considerable disrepair by 1813; but the major repairs then carried out cannot have been substantial enough to withstand the seas to which the dyke was exposed. In earlier years the shoreward end of the dyke had been protected by a field which lay between the end of the dyke and the Mid-rock in Wood haven; but the sea had taken the field away. By about 1831 the dyke had fallen into great disrepair again, and a contract had been let for its restoration. That contract lapsed when the young proprietor, Sir John Carmichael Anstruther, died in a shooting accident at Eton where he was a pupil.

In May 1838 a committee planning harbour improvements recorded that "*a considerable portion of the swarf-dyke and road-way connecting the remnant of the pier from the shore has been washed away during the past winter so as to make the pier insular for an hour or two before and after high water. Several vessels have lately been in the harbour receiving cargoes of coal from Grange Colliery although the carts have to wait for the reflux of tide to get at the pier, or lighters require to be employed to carry the coals to the vessels.*"

In 1842 a petition by some inhabitants of Elie asked the Turnpike Road Trustees to use their funds to repair the road to the harbour. The petitioners declared that the revenue of the Elie Toll bar came mainly from the traffic in the imports and exports of Elie Harbour. They stated that though an agreement had been reached for the repair of the pier the advantages of this would be "in great measure frustrated by the want of a proper road, there being during two or three hours at high water no passage to the harbour and even at low water it is rather a matter of great difficulty to the loaded carts from the point where the road had been ended to the harbour, which is the proper terminus pointed out by the Act (Act Geo IV Cap 84 sec 9)." The Trustees were advised by their clerk that their responsibility for the road would depend on where the landward boundary of the harbour was. If the harbour area was not public property from the Toft up to the landward end of the pier public funds could not be applied to the formation of a road along the swarf. No work was done by the Turnpike Trustees. The titles leave no doubt that the swarf was a part of Elie estate.

In 1847, though by this date the pier had been put into good repair, the Fife Herald reported that "*The Ocean of Glasgow from Stockton, iron and cinders, struck fast on the rocks off Leven, pumped and her afloat she made for Elie. Got in but no help could be given because of the height of the tide nobody could get to the harbour, as the sea forms a complete barrier betwixt it and the town, It is certainly the duties of some parties to put our "Swarf-Dyke" in proper order, and when they fail in doing so, Government, for the preservation of life and property, should certainly interfere.*"

The young Sir John's heir and successor in title had been his uncle, Sir Wyndham Carmichael Anstruther, for whom the estate was latterly administered by trustees. The leading trustee was Henry G. Dickson, WS, of Edinburgh. Administering the estate for an absentee proprietor, Dickson was extremely cautious about spending money on repairs and improvements. Sir Wyndham's entrepreneurial forebears had seen little occasion to spend money on their harbour. His trustees seem to have willing to see it fall down, no doubt motivated in their parsimony by their knowledge of Sir Wyndham's large and growing debts. By 1852, when the trustees were negotiating the sale of his Fife estates to William Baird, their proprietor was in debt in loans secured on the Elie estate to the tune of about £65,000, equivalent to at least £3m today, and possibly on debts secured on his other estates also. Just as at the end of the 16th century and near the end of the 17th century, by the middle of the 19th century a heavily indebted proprietor was obliged to sell the encumbered estate of Elie.

PROPOSALS FOR HARBOUR REPAIRS

During Sir Wyndham's ownership there had been one serious proposal to repair and improve the harbour which in the end the estate had not taken up. In the early 1830s the need to repair the harbour became the subject of a petition to the proprietor signed by 121 inhabitants of Elie. The petition bears no date, but the reference in it to the February gale shows that it was written in 1834, it reads as follows:

Unto Sir Wyndham Carmichael Anstruther Baronet

The Petition of the Inhabitants of Elie

Humbly Sheweth

That your Petitioners have long viewed with much concern the ruinous State of Elie Harbour a port which in Point of natural advantages far surpasses any other in the Frith of Forth.

That it is the opinion of your Petitioners, that were it put into proper repair, it would be the means of saving many lives and much Property That many of the poor fishermen who perished in the dreadful gale of February last year would in all probability have been saved had the Harbour been in a proper State of repair.

That your petitioners consider it to be their duty to acquaint you that the Harbour is held in the highest estimation by every Seafaring man and it is a place of so much importance that your petitioners believe that many individuals might be found willing to risk the necessary outlay provided you were to grant a favourable lease of the Shore dues.

Your petitioners beg also to state that the present ruinous state of the Harbour has been

occasioned by the Pier having been taken down by your late uncle Sir Philip Anstruther who was only prevented by death from carrying his design of rebuilding it into effect.

That your petitioners relying on the goodness of your disposition humbly trust that you will restore their harbour to its former state and by that means restore the now decayed state of trade in the village and neighbourhood besides in some degree enhancing the value of your own estate

That your petitioners earnestly request that you will be pleased to take the subject into your serious consideration.

And your Petitioners will ever Pray &c.

A remarkable feature of the list of signatories, all inhabitants of Elie, is that it includes 30 men described as seamen or sailors, as well as 18 others with occupations connected with the sea, including shipmasters, ship-owners, and Coastguards. Seafaring provided a living for a large proportion of the people of Elie in the 1830s. The next most common occupation is shoemaking, with 13 names, suggesting that there may have been at least one substantial shoemaking business in Elie. With one tannery in Elie and another in Colinsburgh they would not have had far to look for leather.

In the spring of 1836 a new development showed that the petitioners' statement that individuals might be found who would be willing to invest in the harbour was not just a pious hope. A public meeting, largely attended by farmers and landowners as well as others with particular interests in the harbour, was convened to discuss the possibility of improving the harbour. The notice calling the meeting is reproduced as Appendix II.

Writing before the meeting, which took place on May 17, the Fifeshire Journal was optimistic, "*The project is so evidently deserving of support whether viewed as matter of pecuniary speculation, or of solid advantage conferred on the property of the district; and we doubt not that, under the auspices in which the matter has been taken up, the port of Elie will soon be able to boast that it possesses the inestimable advantage of a pier approachable at all times of the tide by the London, Dundee and Aberdeen steam packet, and other vessels of moderate burden.*"

The proprietor was not represented at the meeting, but the trustees for the estate had sent a letter "*giving their full and cordial concurrence to the object of the meeting and stating their readiness to co-operate with the other gentlemen of the county in obtaining an Act of Parliament to enable them to proceed.*" Speakers referred to the great success achieved by the steamboat services to London already started by Dundee and Aberdeen interests for the export of agricultural produce; and the meeting unanimously agreed to support proposals for substantial developments. Subscriptions were readily promised to provide funds to commission a report from the leading engineers Robert Stevenson and Son on the improvement works that would be needed to accommodate the proposed trade.

The report presented by the Stevensons on 23 September 1836 was able to make use of the detailed survey carried out by the senior partner 21 years before. It was submitted to the leading promoters, Sir Ralph Anstruther of Balcaskie, Bart, Mr. Douglas of Grangemuir, elsewhere designated Lord Douglas (he was a son of the Marquess of Queensberry) and others. After making reference to the extent of the anchorage and ease of entering Elie, and to its advantages as a shelter for vessels in the coasting trade when westerly winds prevented them from getting up to Leith, or easterlies prevented them from getting out to sea, the report got down to business. The senior partner's 1815 proposals were sound; but it was recognised funds were limited. The encroachment of sand required the restoration of the pier and of the Swarf Dyke (the Stevensons called it "the Swash Dyke"). To rebuild and widen the outer 70 feet of the pier would cost £1404 12s 4d, a very precisely estimated figure. The Stevensons reported that the paddle steamships to carry export cargoes could not take the ground, and needed a quay which they could "approach during a considerable part of each tide." To provide such a quay in a fully sheltered harbour at Elie would be prohibitively costly. They proposed instead to erect two wharves outside the enclosed harbour, one at Lucky's Hole on the east side of the Law, and thus sheltered from the westerlies, and one on the west side of the Apple Rock with some shelter from the easterlies. They described the proposed wharves as "temporary"; but recommended that in preference to timber structures based on the rock the wharves should be formed by dressing back the

rock as necessary and facing it where required by "*breast walls of masonry protected with defenders of timber.*" Timber wharves would cost nearly as much as those they preferred, which would cost £879 3s 6d for the Apple Rock and £1055 0s 2d for Lucky's Hole. No estimate was given for a proposed cattle pen on the Apple Rock, but that would not be costly. The most expensive part of the scheme was to form a causeway on the line of the Swarf Dyke, with a roadway 20 feet wide and sloping rock taluses where required on either side. This part of the work was costed at £1635 5s 9d making a grand total of £4974 1s 9d.

By 1839 the promoters were able to put formal proposals to the proprietor. They proposed that Sir Wyndham should give up the harbour to a Joint Stock Company to carry out the Stevenson scheme. The capital required by the Company had been estimated at £5,500. The promoters proposed that the estate should be guaranteed an annual payment equivalent to the average revenue it had received in recent years; and the further revenues earned by the Company were to be applied first to the maintenance and management of the harbour. Only after these charges had been met would any dividends be paid to the subscribers to the Company, and these would not exceed 6% on the capital subscribed. The estate would have the right to buy back the harbour after a period of 20 years if the proprietor wished. These seem generous terms, intended to be persuasive, but also indicating that the promoters expected that the farming activities in which they had interests would profit greatly from access to the London market and possibly other markets as well, no matter who owned the harbour.

The estate papers in the Scottish Record Office show that this approach met problems on the estate's side. Because the estate was so heavily encumbered with debt the trustees were not free to grant the kind of lease the Company would require. In the end, nothing came of this very promising scheme in which so many hopes had rested. Partly because the scheme did not proceed, the Stevensons had to wait until April 1838 before, after repeated applications, their reduced bill of £66 was fully paid.

1842 LEASE – THE PIER REPAIRED

It was not until 1842 that a formula was found that

met the legal requirements and enabled the pier at least to be repaired. It reflected the proposals abandoned in 1838 in that it required the proprietor to surrender the revenues of the harbour for a period, in return for having his pier put into repair and an annual payment from the lessees; but this scheme involved no development at all. The only work done was that required to restore the pier. The lease was dated 16 and 18 February 1842. It was granted by Sir Wyndham's Trustees to David Luke, tenant in Newark, John Currie, resident in Elie, and John Currie's son, Thomas. The Curries were successful builders responsible for many of the buildings we see in Elie today. Under its terms the lessees were to put the pier in repair and to maintain it for the 12 year duration of the lease. In return they were granted the right for the period to collect the shore dues and other dues including teind fish and the customs leviable from the *"harbour and Pier and Town of Elie."* The lessees undertook to pay the proprietor £12 per year. The dues were prescribed in the lease and the lessees were forbidden to alter them. The lessees undertook to lay out £220 within 12 months on the repair of the pier to put it into the state in which it had been 35 years before, i.e. one year before the collapse of the pier recorded in 1808. If the lessees had to spend more than £220 to achieve the necessary result this was their responsibility.

David Given, the mason who contracted to carry out the work on behalf of the lessees, stated at a public meeting on 2 December 1848 that he had rebuilt about 75 feet of the pier. This figure corresponds pretty closely with what the Stevenson plan shows and tends to confirm that the 1832 plan does not give an accurate picture of the condition of the pier. Given said that Thomas Currie had paid £240 or £250 for the work, which had been completed about 7 years before, just about the time the lease was signed. It seems possible the lease was simply a formalising of agreements earlier reached and already put into effect. It is the pier as repaired by Given, 170 feet long on its inner face, which is recorded as existing in the plans for the reconstruction of the harbour in 1856 (13). Nothing was done to make good the destroyed Swarf Dyke, which was not mentioned in the 1842 lease.

CONTINUING PROBLEMS
In 1848 Captain Henry Randall, RN, who appears

in the petition of the 1830s as Lieutenant Randall, Commanding Coast Guard, Fife, and two other Elie residents, Dr. Berwick and Mr. James Ovenstone (Pilot, late Merchant) had written to Mr. Dickson to press that the proprietor should rebuild the Sea Wall or Swarf Dyke which they said had been earlier rebuilt by his predecessor. Dickson's reply was that the Trustees could not admit any liability upon the proprietor for the repair of the Dyke "until valid reasons have been assigned for the burden being laid upon him." Dickson may not have looked at the earlier titles, but if he had he would have known that an obligation had been placed upon the proprietor by the 1601 Royal Charter to apply the harbour dues to the maintenance of the three structures it mentions, which include the Swarf Dyke under the designation of "bulwark", His correspondents were not in a position to know of this obligation.

The interesting oil painting by Charles Blyth dated 1848 in the possession of David Thomson, parts of which are reproduced in the cover of this book, shows the harbour from a viewpoint on Elie Ness above the eastern shore of Wood Haven, about where the remaining World War II anti-tank blocks are. It paints the scene perhaps about high water of a neap tide. The line of the Swarf Dyke appears like a series of giant stepping stones being used by two people to get dry-shod to the Law. At full spring tides these stones would be under several feet of water. There is a tall mast on the Law, overtopping the granary by about fifteen feet or so, which could be used to display signals showing the depth of water in the harbour, a paddle steamer in the bay, and a two-masted sailing ship apparently berthing against the quay. Clearly despite its limitations, what Blyth saw was an active harbour.

A newspaper report of April 1849 tells of 20 St. Monans fishing boats that had to run from an easterly gale for shelter in Elie Harbour. They were safe, but the crews were in great danger wading along the submerged swarf to get to safety in the town through waves sweeping in from the east across Wood Haven.

ADMIRALTY COMMISSIONER'S REPORT
Before 1848 there had been so much public concern expressed about the condition of the harbour that the Admiralty appointed a Commissioner to investigate and report. In his 1853 Report, the Commissioner, William Bald, acknowledges in

warm terms the assistance he received from Captain Randall, RN, based at Elie and in command of the Coastguard in Fife. Bald's is a comprehensive and hard-hitting report, placing the blame for the harbour's parlous state firmly on the proprietors. He was clearly unaware of the terms of King James VI's 1601 Charter and the obligation it contained to apply the harbour dues it authorised to be *"employed in building and upholding the haven, shore and bulwark"*; but he conjectured, on the whole correctly, that *"It could never have been the intention of the Crown or meaning of any Grant emanating from it; that a Public Harbour such as Elie, should have been consigned into private hands; the Port dues on shipping converted to private use; the Works of the Harbour left in a state of ruin and allowed to fill several feet up with sand."*

Bald had his key point right. The dues should have been used to maintain all of the three structures that formed the harbour; but the harbour was in fact privately owned though open for public use. If those who received the report had followed up his points they would have found grounds to hold the estate liable to repair the whole of the harbour works; but it does not appear that any effective action followed the report.

A chart prepared by Lieut. T.A. Cudlipp, RN, to accompany Bald's report shows the sandy bed of the main part of the harbour rising at the point of the pier above mean low water springs by about 3 feet, and sloping upwards to the shoreward end of the 1600 quay by about 10 feet more. With a high spring tide of 19 feet or so Cudlipp's contours for the harbour bed nearest the pier and the quay indicate water depths of between 16 and 10 feet.

The figures may be compared with the 22 feet depth reported by the historian Sibbald at the beginning of the 18th century. (Surprisingly, this figure is repeated by the surveyors of the Ordnance Survey in their 1853 records which suggests they had not actually made any depth measurements themselves, but simply written down what they were told.)

It seems likely that the build-up of sand since Sibbald's day explains the difference. It is also possible that Sibbald had recorded the depth of the inner face of the 1600 pier, which was roughly 2 feet higher than the present pier, the masonry face of which down to its base is only 20 feet high.

THE HARBOUR IN 1852

When a deal was struck to sell Sir Wyndham's extensive Fife estates in 1852 to Mr. William Baird the price was £145,000; the old pier and the quay were in a tolerable state of repair; there were some remains showing where the Swarf Dyke had been, but it did not shelter the harbour as it once had; the Law was a tidal islet again; there was considerable accumulation of sand in the harbour; and the roadways along the swarf and in front of the Toft were regularly impassable at high water.

9
Shipping – the coming of steam

SHIPS AND THE CARRYING TRADE

As in earlier years, at the beginning of the 19th century coastwise shipping played a very large part in the transport of goods all round Scotland, particularly heavy and bulky goods. Virtually all sizeable towns and cities were close to the sea or on navigable estuaries. Before heavy industry could be established inland it was necessary to build canals.

Thus harbours like Elie, though small and having only small hinterlands to serve, attracted a steady flow of traffic, carried on entirely in small sailing ships, of which considerable numbers were locally owned. From an entry in the 1817 Topographical Dictionary of Scotland it seems that most of the trade at Elie Harbour may have been in import cargoes. The Dictionary records that the only article of export at the time was grain "*to no great amount*". It appears the granary was not yet attracting a lot of traffic.

These small ships - typical examples are seen in the illustrations (14, 23) - and the larger Elie-owned ships engaged in foreign trade would be crewed largely by local people. In the 1830s there were at least 30 men in Elie (and there would be more in Earlsferry) described as seamen or sailors, and 18 others with occupations connected with the sea. There had been a great increase in the numbers in these occupations since the middle of the 17th century, when at a low period of seafaring activity throughout Scotland Elie was recorded as having only two trading ships of 40 and 50 tons. Alexander Gillespie and other ship-owners of the late 17th century began an expansion in ship owning in Elie which may have reached its peak towards the end of the 18th century or perhaps a little later. The decline thereafter may have been related to the decay of the harbour, but also no doubt the competitive expansion of steamship services in the first half of the century played a large part.

ELIE SHIPS IN THE 1820s

The Anstruther Register of Shipping for the years 1824 to 1826 is preserved in the National Archives of Scotland. It contains the following entries for ships registered to the port of Elie:

Ship	Tonnage	Master	Date of build
1824			
Nancys	58	James Robertson	1819
Pilot	107	John Ovenstone	1814
Union	72	William Sime	1807
1825			
Blues of Elie	108	Philip Blues	1818
Conveyance (Elie-built)	37	Walter Ovenstone	1813
Elizabeth Nairn	41	James Whyte	1825
Euphemia	142	John Millar	1816
Margarets (Elie-built)	55	James Laing	1822
1826			
Mary Laing (Elie-built)	42	James Laing	1814

Without the register for earlier and later years it is not possible to say that this list records all the Elie ships; but with a total tonnage of 662 it shows that the port had at this date a considerable merchant fleet. There are three ships of over 100 tons, comparable in size to the seven foreign-going ships of Elie recorded in the Statistical Account of 1796.

The names James Robertson and John Ovenstone appear, with the designation "Ship Owner" among the signatories of the 1834 petition later described, as well as that of John Ovenston, with the designation "Pilot". One of the Ovenston(e)s may have been master of the ship "Pilot" registered in 1824.

ELIE SHIPS IN 1852

Despite the very poor access to the harbour in 1852 there were still several ships registered by owners giving Elie as their home port. Lists of registered shipping on the east coast of Scotland show an interesting pattern. For Leith itself, including the creeks of Granton, Fisherrow, Cockenzie, and Dunbar, the total number of ships is 175, and the total tonnage 24,392 tons, averaging 139 tons. Dundee had a much bigger fleet, 360 ships of 60,000 tons in all, averaging 167 tons, while Aberdeen had the largest ships, averaging 234 tons.

In the East Neuk, Crail had 15 ships, of 734 tons, averaging 48 tons, and Elie 4 of 155 tons, averaging 39. The Elie list reads as follows.

Year (built)	Names	Masters	Owners	Tons
1834	*Isabella*	Dick	Elie & Leith Shipping Co	45
1845	*Paragon*	McRuvie	Mary Millar and Steel	33
1817	*Annie*	McRuvie	D. McRuvie	34
1815	*Guthries*	Smith	R. Smith	43

This list shows a sad decline from the flourishing merchant fleet of the 1790s. It also shows that the size of ships engaged principally if not exclusively in the coastal trade did not change, limited as it was by the capacity of the small harbours they had to use, in the Forth and the Tay Estuaries and elsewhere.

The Parochial Directory of 1861 records 7 shipmasters, 3 of whom lived in South Street, 2 in the High Street, and 2 in Park Place. Locally-owned ships would not carry all of the harbour's trade, but must have taken a good share of the main export cargoes of grain, potatoes, and livestock. Their import cargoes included articles of merchandise for shopkeepers; furniture and other bulky items for householders, and goods required by local industries, builders, farmers and craftsmen, of which hides and bark for tanning formed a large part.

Some bulk cargoes, like lime required for agriculture and building work, would possibly have been available more cheaply when shipped by sea from Limekilns than when carted overland from kilns elsewhere in Fife. Lime from the Earl of Elgin's lime works at Limekilns was shipped in vessels which specialised in that hazardous trade: it was shipped in the form of quicklime which re-acted dangerously when brought into contact with water.

THE COMING OF STEAM

Sailing ships retained an important share of the coastal and other trades for much of the 19th century and were not wholly displaced by steamer services for many years into the 20th century. The first steamship seen on the Forth was Henry Bell's famous *Comet*, of Helensburgh, which he brought by the canal from the Clyde to the Forth in 1813. The shape of things to come was shown almost at once, when Bell began running excursions for passengers between Leith and Bo'ness at a one-way fare of 7s 6d. The *Comet* was soon followed by steamships designed for what had become their most important early use. This was to serve as auxiliaries for the large established merchant fleets of sailing ships, by towing ships arriving in the roads to berths in the main ports, and helping them leave harbour as required. The noun "*tug*" itself comes from the name of a vessel built for this service by Denny of Dumbarton in 1817. The first "tug" was built for service on the Forth to tow ships between Leith and Bo'ness and to the eastern end of the Forth-Clyde canal near Grangemouth.

While waiting for trade the early tugs could add to their revenues by offering short pleasure trips. From these simple beginnings the great excursion steamer trade developed on the Forth as well as the Clyde and reliable ferry services followed, though sailing packets continued in service as ferries for a considerable time.

At the same time the value of steamships as cargo carriers was quickly appreciated. As early as 1826 the Forth saw in service between Leith and London the largest steamship yet, 160 feet in length, built in Greenock. By 1836, as noted earlier, the advantages of the steamship had become apparent to the landowners and farmers of the East Neuk. Impressed by the service offered by the London, Dundee and Aberdeen steam packet, their consortium saw the possibilities of developing the harbour of Elie to enable them to sell their produce in the London market. This came to nothing; and there seems to be no record of the first steamship to call at Elie.

STEAMER SERVICES AT ELIE

A good impression of how steamer services at Elie developed is given in "*The New Statistical Account of Scotland*", compiled, like the pioneering Statistical Account of the 1790s, from parish accounts prepared by the parish Ministers. The Elie account, contributed by the Rev. George Milligan, is dated December 1836. His notes deserve to be quoted in full:

"*MEANS OF COMMUNICATION - There is a post-office in the village. It is a sub-office to that at Colinsburgh. The post arrives at eight every morning, and departs betwixt six and seven in the evening. Much might be done for equalizing the rates of postage - great anomalies existing in that respect. A turnpike road runs through the whole extent of the parish. Toll-bars in abundance. If I go to Pittenweem, a distance of four miles, I have two to pay. If I travel in the opposite direction to Kirkcaldy, I have three; whereas the neighbouring parish to the east, though at a greater distance, has only two. There is a coach that Passes and repasses daily in connection with the steamboat betwixt Largo and Newhaven. But the great channel of communication is the sea. We have two regular packets that sail weekly to Leith exporting the produce of the land, and importing those articles of merchandise which are required for the consumption of the Neighbourhood. Steam, however, is the chief agent, and nothing has done more for opening up the coast of Fife than the application of it to sailing vessels. Besides the boat already mentioned, which in summer sails twice a day from the Chain Pier at Trinity to Largo, the Aberdeen and Dundee steam-vessels daily vist us twice, and occasionally three times, both going and returning. And were the harbour repaired, it is supposed that a direct steam communication would be established betwixt this place and London.*"

Mr. Milligan's account also contains some pointed comments about the number of houses where "*spiritous liquors were being retailed*". When he came to the parish there were eleven, by December 1836 he was proud to have managed to persuade the magistrates to reduce the number of licences to five: four grocers and one inn. This clearly gave him some satisfaction, but it was not good enough. The first record of a licence for the

Ship Inn, in the Toft near the harbour, which from that date to this has played an important part in the life of the harbour community, is found in 1838. Here perhaps Mr. Milligan may have begun to lose ground in face of the increasing harbour traffic he describes.

The "*two regular packets*" sailing weekly to Leith could easily be provided by a single cargo-carrying sailing ship, possibly a successor to the sloop engaged in the coasting trade recorded in the 1790s, which was a sailing vessel of moderate size based in Elie. For local passenger traffic steamer services were now available, provided by the passing steamers which ran daily services between Granton and Aberdeen and Dundee, as well as the regular ferry from Largo Pier (L.Pr on the milestones of the period) to the Chain Pier at Newhaven.

These services are also described by Leighton in his history of Fife published in 1840. He records the remarkable frequency of steamboat services available to Elie travellers in the summer. Later in the decade a statement by the agent for the Aberdeen Leith and Clyde Steamship Company showed that by the mid-1840s their Aberdeen vessels called at Elie twice daily for nine months of the year. Leighton also notes that "*The coach from St. Andrews to Largo passes regularly through Elie every day during the summer, to meet the steamboat for Newhaven.*" It was these services made possible the rapid development of Elie as a holiday resort.

Some details of how the services continued to develop are to be found in a notice (11) published in Dundee by the Edinburgh and Dundee Steam-Packet Company in September 1845, and their advertisements in the East Fife newspapers. The Dundee notice was of course designed to attract local passengers. The last part of the notice draws attention to connecting services that would be important to some Dundee businessmen and others.

The speed of Mr. Denny's "*fine new iron steamer*" that is indicated by the timetable is impressive. The distance from Granton Pier to Dundee Harbour is approximately 57 nautical miles. Even allowing as little as 5 minutes delay for each of the three intermediate off-shore calls, the notice shows that the *Britannia* was expected to average over 16 knots on the passage. It seems likely this would be achieved only when conditions were reasonably favourable. At most Fife harbours in the earlier period of paddle steamer services, in the absence of piers suitable for the ships to come alongside, the passengers were carried by "*flory-boats*" to the steamers lying offshore.

In 1846 a similar service was provided by the *Benledi*, built by Robert Barclay of Glasgow. Experience with the service these ships had provided no doubt led to the major change and new investment made in the service in 1847. On May 1 the Company advertised "Daily Steam Conveyance to and from Edinburgh and Dundee", provided by the "fine new iron steamers" - a description the Company clearly liked - *Bold Buccleuch* (Captain P. Greig, 209 tons) and *Earl of Rosslyn* (Captain David Adamson, 191 tons). With these two ships the company ran a service providing a single passage in each direction daily. The morning departures were from Dundee at ten and from Granton at half-past ten, the times being chosen to connect with the limited rail service at both cities, as well as with coach services at Dundee. The notice indicated that the vessels would call off Elie, Anstruther, and Crail, weather permitting, as the *Britannia* had done.

The change suggests that the earlier timetable, with its short turn-round at Dundee had not been as suitable either for passengers or for cargo-handling as had been hoped. A service which meant at least one overnight stay for the return passenger was more realistic; and the ships' overnight stays at both ports meant there was plenty of time for the loading and discharge of cargo.

In the 1850s the steamer *Xanthe* (62 tons) provided regular packet services between Anstruther and Leith, which included calls at Elie, Largo, Leven and Dysart. By 1855 Elie was the only intermediate port of call. The railway had reached Leven by 1854, and was extended to Kilconquhar Station in 1857. In 1856 the *Xanthe* was replaced by the *Forth* (138 tons) which continued the service summer and winter until 1875, latterly mainly as a cargo-carrier. By this date the railway was carrying almost all the passenger traffic (excursion cruises excepted). A cargo service operated by the screw steamer *Cameo* (60 tons) continued for a further two years; but by the 1880s the trade in cargoes of goods for local consumption had mostly passed to the railway, which had been extended from Kilconquhar to Anstruther by 1863. From about 1880 the main cargo traffic at the harbour, most of it probably still carried by small sailing ships, was in the products of the local farms, mainly to harbours elsewhere in the United Kingdom, though on occasion merchant skippers from continental ports would pick up cargoes of potatoes. The farmers' need to change their potato seed from time to time would perhaps be a factor in this export trade.

NAVIGATIONAL AIDS

The coming of frequent steamship services seems to have sharpened concerns about local dangers to navigation. The harbour at Elie is not difficult to enter, because it has an open approach through the wide stretch of water between the Thill Rock and the pier; but there are hazards not far away along the coast in both directions. In addition to the obvious dangers presented by the rocks and skerries of Elie Ness, Elie Law, Chapel Ness and Kincraig, there are reefs stretching out from the shore, particularly near Chapel Ness, and four notable off-lying rocks. These are the Ox Rock, a little east of Elie Ness, the Thill Rock, in the middle of the bay, the East Vows to the south-east of Chapel Ness, and the West Vows off Chapel Ness to the south-west. The first three of these rocks are in positions which make them particular dangers to ships sailing along the coast, and especially to those entering Elie.

The seamen and fishermen who frequented Elie bay in earlier centuries would have their familiar marks to guide them safely past these hazards. The Law and later the pier and later still the granary would be important marks, combining with the conspicuous buildings of the town behind to give a useful choice of bearings for an approaching vessel.

One of the stories handed down of an early navigation aid should perhaps be treated with some caution. It is said that the ferries that crossed from North Berwick in medieval times were guided when overtaken by the dark by a lamp shown in a window in one of the hospice buildings on Chapel Ness, and also that traces of a lamp fitting were to be seen in the ruins for many years after the hospice was deserted. This is not totally unlikely. The entrance channel to the ferry pier at Chapel Ness is narrow. More help would be needed to get in to the pier on a really dark night than a single light in a hospice window; but it is not at all difficult to envisage circumstances in which a light could provide a vital steer for a pilgrim ferry.

We do not know when the first signal mast was erected on Elie Law, but the one which we do know about was certainly in place in the first half of the 19th century. It was a navigation aid on which flag or other signals could be made to ships intending to enter Elie, to give them information and in particular to let them know the depth of water inside the pier.

Elie Harbour was for centuries a place to which ships and fishing-boats not infrequently ran for shelter. Wrecks were not uncommon, and in the early part of the 19th century, particularly when steam vessels began to call several times a week, and eventually daily, pressure grew for the worst dangers to be marked.

It was therefore not surprising that in his 1841 Report to the Commissioners of Northern Lighthouses their engineer Robert Stevenson included the recommendation "*The Vows Rocks which lie within half a mile of Ely Harbour near the mouth of the Firth half tide rocks to be marked with a Spur Beacon of Iron*". This beacon would effectively protect ships against two hazards at once, by clearly marking the east Vows and also by providing a mark for an easy sailing direction to avoid the Ox Rock, which though near the surface is actually under water for most of each tide. The direction in the Admiralty Chart is very simple "*Vows Beacon open of Elie Ness clears the Ox Rock*".

The Commissioners required the approval of Trinity House, the old established lighthouse authority in London, to carry out a work of this kind. After an inspection by the Elder Brethren of Trinity House that approval was withheld. The Elder Brethren took the view that "*the immediate contiguity*" of the rock to the shore made a beacon unnecessary. The rock is in fact separated from the shore at low water springs by some fair distance.

After five wrecks, some with loss of life, and several memorials pressing for the Vows to be marked, Trinity House finally gave way. Work was started on the massive six-legged iron beacon in March 1847 and completed by 23 September. The upper part of the beacon is so designed as to provide a "chair of refuge" in which 8 or 10 persons shipwrecked on the rock could if necessary find a rather uncomfortable place of

safety above the reach of the sea. In January 1848 the Commissioners published a Notice to Mariners announcing the establishment and the position of the beacon, and also of a large black buoy which they had put in place to mark the Thill Rock. Those two marks made Elie Bay a very much safer harbour for shipping.

A further navigation mark was added by the second William Baird who had succeeded his father in 1864. This was a white light fixed on a hollow iron column (2, 14, 25) erected on the end of the pier in 1868. The column contained a gas plant using calcium carbide and water to generate the acetylene which fuelled the light.

At some date, perhaps at the time the pier head light was installed, an inner leading mark to be used in conjunction with the light on the pier was erected in the garden of what was then the manse in the eastern section of the Terrace. This defined a line for a safe approach to the pier which would comfortably clear the Apple Rock. There is no record of whether this mark was ever lit, but it could easily have been. A light might have been set on it by arrangement on occasions of special need. Elie Ness Lighthouse was not installed till the 20th century.

EXCURSION CRUISES

Excursion cruises on the Forth began with the arrival of the first steam tugs, initially it appears on a fairly irregular basis, depending on the demands for their services in their primary role. In 1854 a dedicated excursion and towing business was set up by Donald R. Macgregor, a Leith businessman, and Captain John Galloway, a former shipmaster. Regular scheduled excursions to Elie seem to have begun about 1873, just about the time the steam packet service from Anstruther was coming to an end, no doubt because of competition from the railway. The new excursions were provided by ships which were still primarily tugs, the *William Scott* (78 tons) and the *Integrity* (80 tons). From 1877 there were regular excursions to Elie and North Berwick by the *Fiery Cross* (87 tons), a former tug nicknamed the "*Floatin' Shebeen*", owned by George Jamieson. She had little passenger accommodation. Obviously this included a popular bar but she was faster than her competitors and aggressively promoted. On her final voyage of each season she mounted a large blazing wooden cross on the top of her mizzen mast. Her principal competitors were two saloon steamers launched in 1874 for John Ridd, a Leith wine merchant. The *Lord Elgin* and the *Lord Mar*, each of 203 tons, were licensed to carry 715 passengers. They were slower, but had better passenger accommodation than the *Fiery Cross*, and provided twice-weekly cruises to Elie.

After two years of disappointing results the *Lord Elgin* was sold for service on the south coast of England in 1881. She continued in service, latterly as a cargo carrier, until 1953, 77 years after she was launched. The *Lord Mar* had also been sold. Not long after the sale of these two fine ships the excursion trade took off, with the introduction of the *Carrick Castle* (176 tons, 192 feet) which the Glasgow firm of Matthew and Mathieson brought to the Forth. She was an instant success, the fastest passenger ship yet seen on the Forth, able to reach Elie from Leith in little over an hour, and from Portobello Pier in even less time, much faster than the train service of the day. Her speed made extended cruises possible. In one year the regular Thursday cruise went round the Bass, the May Island and the Bell Rock. In 1884 the Thursday cruise went to Berwick-upon-Tweed, leaving Leith at 9 a.m. and returning at 8.30 p.m. In that same year the Wednesday cruise allowed passengers a long afternoon ashore in Elie, from 12 noon to 6.30 p.m.

VISITS OF THE CHANNEL FLEET

Apart from the various guard ships that were stationed off North Queensferry, the Royal Navy was not seen in the Forth for decades after the end of the Napoleonic wars. In 1860 this changed, with a visit from the Channel Fleet, which lasted from 9 June to 23 June. During most of that time the Fleet was at anchor in St. Margaret's Hope near Rosyth. (The naval dockyard was not built until the 20th century.) The visit caused great excitement locally. The interest was such that all the steamships on the Forth and many from further afield were diverted from their usual services for much of the fortnight to carry passengers to see the Fleet.

Visits were made in 1861 and for a number of years thereafter. In 1867 the East of Fife Record reported that on July 29 the Channel Fleet "*this squadron of splendid war vessels*" passed up the Firth on the way to Leith. In that year the flagship was the *Warrior*, the first of the ironclads, which can still be seen, in impeccable condition, close to Nelson's *Victory* in Portsmouth Dockyard.

The *Warrior*, launched in 1860, set new standards for battleships, with armour protecting its large central "citadel" which no gun of the day could pierce, a speed under sail and steam combined which could reach 17.5 knots, 2 knots faster than any other contemporary warship, and the most powerful guns yet seen at sea, including 10 110-pounders. She displaced 9,210 tons. It was not surprising she was the ship all the visitors wanted to see: so great were the crowds that at the end of one day the returning ferries and other small craft had to leave some of the visitors to spend the night on board.

The Record of August 8 carries a report of the fleet lying off Elie, mustering for the return south. The Record's Elie correspondent reported "*Our shore was lined with spectators, the regular inhabitants being greatly increased by our numerous summer visitors. Telescopes of every shape and size were in requisition, and it was somewhat amusing to listen to the various observations*". Clearly the Record's correspondent was rather a superior person.

In that same year the Harbour Master of Elie found his name in the Record. It reported that on October 31 Peter Simpson and his grandson were on the Fish Rocks (the rocks at the point now called Elie Ness), when the boy fell into the water. The elderly harbour master threw off his coat, plunged in and with considerable difficulty managed to get the boy and himself out of the water and up the high and steep face of the rock.

10

William Baird's harbour development

WILLIAM BAIRD - THE NEW PROPRIETOR

The sale of Sir Wyndham's extensive Fife estates to William Baird was legally completed in 1853. Baird was possibly the most successful Scottish industrialist of the period. At the age of twenty, in the year 1816, he had become the manager of a colliery newly-opened by his father near Airdrie; and with his father and brothers he opened a series of pits in the area, engaging in canal building and operating a fleet of canal boats to deliver coal to Glasgow. Later they invested in railways for the same (and wider) purposes. In the year 1828 the Bairds became ironmasters, leasing mineral rights to the ironstone deposits near their collieries, and opening their first blast furnace at Gartsherrie near Airdrie in 1830. The Bairds were among the pioneers in the commercial use of the hot blast process invented by J. B. Neilson in 1828. They had 16 blast furnaces operating by 1842, capable of producing more than 100,000 tons of iron per year. In 1844 they expanded into Ayrshire, ultimately operating there on an even larger scale, with coalpits, ironstone workings, and 26 blast furnaces. By 1868 the Baird Company was the largest iron-producing company in Scotland, producing 300,000 tons of pig iron a year, a quarter of the entire Scottish production.

William had taken over the business on his father's death in 1833, and it became "William Baird and Company". He was the MP for Falkirk Burghs from 1841 to 1846, chairman of the Caledonian Railway Company, and a director and later governor of the Forth and Clyde Canal. Having played such a large part in the later stages of the Industrial Revolution in Scotland, he must have seen the problems and opportunities presented by his newly-acquired small and dilapidated harbour of Elie as pretty small concerns. Perhaps they provided him with some relaxation from the work involved in directing his enormous enterprises in Lanarkshire and Ayrshire, a kind of hobby investment.

BAIRD'S HARBOUR WORKS: THE FIRST STAGES

Although the old pier had been put into good repair in 1842 the rest of the structure was ruinous. The Ordnance Survey map (12) of 1854 (which was based on survey work done in 1853) shows the island harbour of Elie with no connections to the shore, except some indication of where the swarf was, shown as a broken line of tidal reefs. The O.S. surveyors' report describing the harbour is reproduced as Appendix II. It is as if the swarf dyke and the roadway alongside it had never been: there is no suggestion in the map that the fairly regular line of large rocks shown in the 1848 painting, that appear to be a remnant of the swarf dyke, were still in place. In addition to the problems caused by the lack of a proper access road, part of the quay wall in front of the granary had fallen in.

The first requirement for the improvement of the harbour was to restore the access road. Part of this would have to be formed by making a serviceable public road out of the narrow lane (10) running between the houses of the Toft and their sea gardens to reach the landward end of the swarf. This would replace the road along the shore in front of the sea gardens which had been completely swept away. Between the end of the sea gardens and the foot of Stenton Row the new road would require a substantial sea wall to be built to support it and protect it from the sea. This would cut across the remains of the sloping ways down which the shipyard had launched its ships. The roadway along the swarf would have to be constructed by the proprietor.

Initially however, Baird chose to follow the well-tried route of stressing the harbour's value as a harbour of refuge, with its reputation borne out by past and also recent experience. This led him to think that before considering what he himself might do with the harbour, in its prevailing state more of a liability than an asset, he might be able to hand it over to a public authority. He was prompted to take early action on this by a letter from a Royal Commission, enquiring into the local charges upon shipping, requesting information from him about the charges made at his harbour. He would not be impressed by what he found out about the harbour's revenues, and he knew that much expensive work would be needed to put it into good working order and to attract more traffic.

Accordingly, he wrote to the First Lord of the Admiralty on 21 October 1853, pointing out the importance of Elie as a harbour of refuge "much needed on this part of the coast" and "*called for by a prevailing clamour*". Having emphasized the public benefits that would flow from the repair and improvement of the harbour, he went on to offer to transfer it to the ownership of the Admiralty or any public authority they might nominate: later papers relating to Baird's Elie Harbour Bill of 1857 show that he received a dusty answer.

He had probably anticipated this, because about the same time he began discussions with the Turnpike Trustees for the St. Andrews District about the road to the harbour. On 9 May 1854 they considered a letter from Baird, in which he offered to build and maintain the necessary sea wall if the Trustees would build and maintain the road leading to the harbour, which meant the road leading as far as the landward end of the swarf. The Trustees agreed to proceed with the formation of the road, and approved the plans submitted by their surveyor, who estimated the cost of forming the road by the Trustees at £661 18s 1d.

Immediately the Trustees had approved the essential public road works Baird acted to put into effect the substantial scheme he had already planned to form an access road from the end of the turnpike road along the swarf to the Law. In October 1853, at about the time he was writing to the Admiralty, he had received preliminary sketch plans from his civil engineer, John Moffat of Ardrossan, for a "New Approach" and a new pier. Baird at the time had his private residence at Rosemount near Ayr, and no doubt had experience of Moffat's work in connection with his extensive Ayrshire enterprises. Moffat's letters to Baird show that he enjoyed his employer's full confidence. It is clear from Moffat's letters about these plans that the pier plan he had prepared at that stage was much less ambitious than the one Baird ultimately implemented; but the "new approach" designed by Moffat appears to be the causeway Baird had built in 1854. We do not have contract documents

or accounts to show what the work cost.

The invitation to contractors to tender for the approach road works was dated 22 May 1854, the tenders had to be submitted by 3 June, and the whole of the work was to be finished by 1 October. Such a timetable would be unimaginable today; and it clearly proved to be over-ambitious then. No doubt it reflects the pace at which Baird was accustomed to drive his industrial projects in the West. Baird entered into a contract for the work with Kenneth Mathieson, Junior, a Dunfermline contractor, on 14 July 1854. A press report of 5 May 1855 shows how far behind schedule the project fell. "*Elie. The seawall leading to the harbour is now finished. Road metal has to be laid to complete the work. The wall has a very neat appearance but fears are entertained that sand is depositing in the harbour. Should the sand increase a breakwater is proposed to be erected.*"

As a condition of tendering, contractors had to undertake to uphold the whole work for a period of five years for an annual payment to be specified in the tender. As a means of preventing poor workmanship this condition could hardly be bettered.

The line laid down for the new causeway largely followed that of the collapsed Swarf Dyke, and the plans were backed by carefully detailed specifications. These provided that the foundation courses for the two parallel sea walls protecting the roadway (to be about 21 feet wide) were to be of very large stones of defined size and thickness "*to be got from the beach opposite Elie and Earlsferry*". Only the eastern wall is now visible, rising generally about 17 feet above the rocky shore. The backing of the walls was to be of "*heavy substantial rubble got from Ardross or from the Beach opposite Elie and Earlsferry, and laid in courses with the Ashlar*". The present condition of the causeway testifies to the enduring value of this specification.

The causeway, 460 feet long, leads to a widened and lengthened quay of 600 feet stretching in front of the Law and the Granary to the root of the pier. This quay must have been the subject of a separate and later contract. It is clear from the comments dated 12 May 1857 by the Admiralty on Baird's Elie Harbour Bill of that year that the quay had been completed by that date. Thus even before the pier had been improved, Baird had re-created in greatly improved form the main parts of the structure which were needed for commercial shipping operations.

Having failed to persuade the Admiralty that his harbour should be in public ownership Baird made one further attempt to obtain financial help from the Government. He sent a memorial "To the Honourable the Commissioners of the Board of British White Herring Fishery". He went into considerable detail to explain the need for a safe harbour of refuge on the Firth of Forth for the large fishing fleets based there, and the suitability of Elie harbour for this purpose. He said he was willing to give "*liberal assistance*" to such a scheme. This more persuasive approach than the first, rather bald, letter he had earlier sent to the Admiralty proved equally ineffectual.

ELIE HARBOUR BILL 1857

Nothing remained but to continue the work at his own expense, and because this would involve development in navigable waters he required to promote a Private Bill to obtain Parliamentary approval. This was understandably well-supported by local interests, as shown, for example, by a Petition to Parliament from "proprietors, agriculturalists, and traders in the districts of Colinsburgh and Kilconquhar". Their petition states "*That from the District they occupy large quantities of potatoes, wheat, and other agricultural produces and fat cattle are exported*" and "*That the Port of Elie formerly afforded the means of shipment for the district within convenient distance, but for some years bygone it has fallen into decay, and your Petitioners are compelled to transmit their Farm Produce by a long and Expensive land Carriage to other and more distant points*".

Baird's draft bill sought authority to build to a more ambitious plan, designed for him by Moffat, than the one that he was eventually authorised to carry out. There is an acerbic tone to the exchanges between Baird and the Admiralty in the memoranda relating to the Bill. The Admiralty's initial report to Parliament was rather hostile and elicited some testy but well-founded comments from Baird. The Admiralty expressed doubts about the extent of the area included in Baird's title to "the port and haven of Elie". Baird's reply referred them to the Royal Charters; and he won most of the disputed points. The matter was resolved by the Admiralty accepting a much wider title than they were at first

prepared to recognise, and Baird agreeing that the outer part of the bay was not part of the harbour proper but was controlled by him as an anchorage only. The relevant section of the 1857 Act reads as follows:

"Limits of Elie Harbour

IV. The Limits of the Harbour of *Elie* shall be deemed and are hereby declared to be a straight Line drawn from the Southern Extremity of *Elie Ness* on the East to the Boundary at High-water Mark, between the Properties of the said *William Baird* and the Burgh of *Earlsferry* on the West, and which line is laid down and marked A.B.C. on the Plan of the Harbour deposited at the Admiralty Office, *Whitehall*, and the Harbour shall extend to and include the whole Space within the said Limits; and the Limits of the Anchorage adjoining the Harbour shall be deemed and are hereby declared to be a straight Line drawn from the Southern Extremity of *Elie Ness* on the East to the Rocks called *Vows*, and another straight Line from the said Rocks to *Chapel Ness* on the West, and which Lines are also laid down on the said Plan deposited at the Admiralty Office, and marked A.D. and D.E."

BAIRD'S MODIFIED SCHEME

The Admiralty declined to approve one very large element in Baird's plan, which he was obliged to abandon. The part he did carry out was to build a new and larger pier (2,13), 230 feet in length and thus 70 feet longer than the old pier, but also wider and slightly lower. The engineering drawings show that only the upper layer of the old pier was to be removed. The old structure below the surface of the new pier forms the core of the present structure up to 160 feet from the root of the pier.

The pier was to be of the same substantial construction as the causeway. The outer face was to be of Queensferry whinstone but the inner and end faces were to be of Burntisland sandstone. Both have weathered very well. The plan provided for the in-fill "*hearting*" to be excavated from Elie Law, which had the added benefit of widening the flat area behind the quay.

The part of the plan that Baird was obliged to give up was a proposed breakwater 700 feet long projecting from the shore at the foot of School Wynd (then called Auchmuty Wynd) to line up with the outer end of the pier, leaving an entrance 180 feet wide. The Admiralty doubted if shelter

ELIE

Shepherd Law

Sauchar Point

Bathinghouse

Elie Ness

Wood Haven

Elie Harbour Pier

EARLSFERRY

Chapel Ness

Quarry

Spring

Earlsferry House

Chapel Ness

East Vows

Chair of Metage

12. 6-inch Ordnance Survey Map - 1854

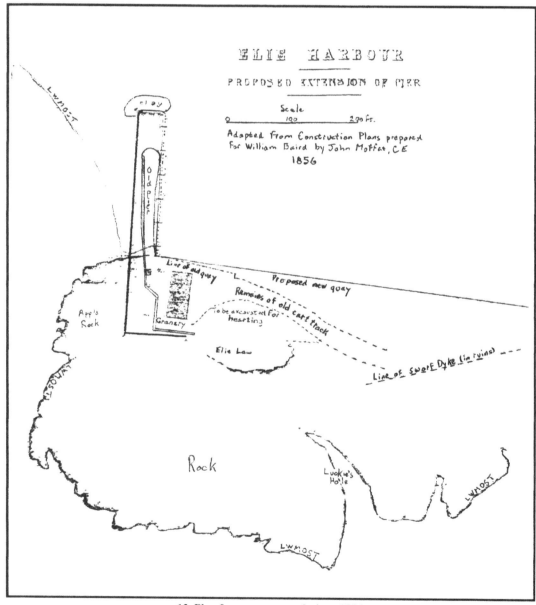

13. Plan for new quay and pier - 1856

was required from the direction protected by the proposed breakwater, an objection in which there is clearly some force; but they also suggested that if it was built "*it might increase the tendency of the harbour to sand up*". From the press report of May 1855 referred to above it appears Baird saw the breakwater as a means of preventing or limiting the deposition of sand. The Admiralty's contrary view seems to have been profoundly mistaken. In the event, the rapid and continuing deposition of sand in the harbour which immediately followed the building of the causeway and the extension of the pier is hard to explain except in terms of the visible tidal currents which carry sand from the beach in front of the town into the harbour and deposit it in the slack water contained between the Toft, the causeway, and the pier. It seems most unlikely that a harbour entrance only 180 feet wide, pointing directly out into the Firth, would have allowed such sand-bearing tidal currents to flow into the harbour.

It is an indication of how serious Baird's interest was that he was prepared to carry out so large a scheme. The estimated cost of the works in Moffat's original plan was certified to Parliament as £16,000, the greater part of which would have been required for the west breakwater. The total cost of the pier enlargement, with some minor remedial work needed on the new quay, was £5,861 5s 10d. The contractors were John and Allan Granger and James Ewen, who signed a formal contract with Baird on 30 August 1859, by which date the work was already well under way.

On 28 May the East of Fife Record had reported great activity on the building of the new pier, and also that "*At the same time large quantities of potatoes are being shipped while other vessels are loading iron stones several hundred tons of which are lying in the harbour ready for shipment. All these together with our usual packet traffic causes great stir and apparent confusion*". Elie Harbour was a very busy place in 1859; and it appears that Baird's earlier work in creating a proper access road and lengthening the quay was already showing results, even before the pier had been improved.

The pier was of course not available for cargo-handling while the old pier was being demolished and the widened pier built; but by 11 February 1860 a large section of the new pier was open to traffic, though the extension to lengthen the pier from 160 to 230 feet had still to be built. This work appears to have begun that month, and almost immediately the East of Fife Record had to report a sad accident. On 2 March "*Thomas Sim, mason, working at the new works at the harbour, several tons of stone fell on him when a prop was accidentally banged, instantaneous death. Aged 33*". He may have been of the same family as the Simes, whose occupations are given as masons, and who signed the 1830s petition asking the proprietor of the estate pressing for the harbour to be put into repair.

In May the Record reported that the work on the extension was going on day and night (clearly to take advantage of every low tide) and that the contractors hoped to finish soon. The whole work seems to have taken about a year. It was a requirement in the 1857 Act that the completion of the work had to be formally certified. Accordingly, the Sheriff Substitute of Fife at Cupar came to Elie on July 28. On that day he inspected the work, took depositions from Thomas Currie, Architect, Elie, who had been superintendent of the work, and Andrew Wilkie, Writer, Leven, who had been Baird's agent, and duly certified that the pier had been completed on accordance with the Act.

House of Commons interest

In August 1857, only days after the passing of the Elie Harbour Bill, a committee of the House of Commons considering the need for breakwaters and harbours of refuge for the fishing fleets on the east coast of Scotland recommended several proposals to the House. These were to build two breakwaters at Wick at a cost of £175,175; a harbour at Peterhead, at a cost of £227,905; two breakwaters at Elie, at a cost of £200,000; and a breakwater at Dunbar at a cost of £150,000. It is apparent from the figures that the proposals for Wick and Peterhead had been planned in some detail, while those for Elie and Dunbar were the subject of preliminary estimates only. The high cost of the Elie proposal shows that a very extensive scheme had been devised. There exists a print of Cudlipp's chart of 1853 which shows two planned major extensions to enclose a very large area of deep water. There can be little doubt that this plan was drawn to provide the basis for the Committee's estimate. It shows two breakwaters designed to enclose the whole of Elie Bay from Elie Ness to Chapel Ness, with a wide opening appropriate for a harbour of refuge. The Elie Ness breakwater was to be 900 feet long, projecting roughly west and the Chapel Ness breakwater 1600 feet long, projecting in a generally east-south-easterly direction, from the skerries off Chapel Ness, which include rocks called the Inner Vows, to near the Thill Rock, with a change of direction part way along to line up the ends of the two structures. Wood Haven had long been regarded as the most promising site to enclose as a harbour of refuge, but this was a far more ambitious scheme.

In the event nothing came of the proposal. No doubt Baird had been instrumental in getting it before the Committee, but once again he was to be disappointed. Nothing was done at Elie. Some work was carried out at Dunbar, which the Fishery Board designated as the harbour of refuge for all the fishing fleets of the Forth. The substantial breakwater built at Wick was damaged in severe storms between 1870 and 1872, the damage culminating in the astonishing displacement of a section of the breakwater estimated to weigh 1350 tons.

POTENTIAL FOR HARBOUR-RELATED DEVELOPMENTS

Baird's ambitions, and the reasons for the willingness of this successful entrepreneur to invest so heavily in his harbour, may be reflected in a revealing editorial and article in the East Fife Record of August 29, 1857. The editorial begins very sombrely, reviewing the latest news of the Indian Mutiny. It then reports that the general opinion on the recently passed Scottish Bills (a Police Bill and a Lunacy Bill) is that they would involve needless expenditure and "*be chiefly useful for providing snug sinecures for a few Government supporters*".

The editorial is followed by an article attributed to the Fifeshire Journal, which discusses in detail the possibilities opened up by the development of the Elie Harbour, particularly with the recently-completed extension of the East of Fife Railway to Kilconquhar. It describes the special advantages presented by a commercial harbour near the entrance to the Firth of Forth and thus more quickly reached by incoming ships meeting the winds usually prevailing than harbours further up the Firth; and it goes on: "*The projected works*

are to be on an extensive scale …. We cannot also overlook the fact that, commensurate with the extension of the harbour there are facilities for the erection of warehouses, foundries, dockyards and other appurtenances to a commercial haven; the extensive links to the eastward of Elie, now used as a rabbit warren, affording feus not only for such buildings, but for the dwelling-houses and especially for the cabins of the seamen and fishermen whom we hope to find attracted from the neighbouring ports of Cellardyke and St. Monance, and settled in this more salubrious and convenient locality".

The article continues in this vein for some length, and sheds some light on what Baird might have had in mind when he undertook such substantial works to improve a harbour which before his time had had only the trade which a small and almost exclusively agricultural hinterland could support.

We do know that Baird had in mind at least one further project for the development of the harbour. When he bought the Anstruther estates he was aware that there were extensive coal workings on his newly-acquired properties; and he commissioned a survey of one area which he presumably thought particularly promising, the Pittenweem Coalfield, to determine whether it was worth developing. One of the reasons for his massive harbour works, with the wide roadway and wide pier was that he at one time contemplated using the harbour for the shipping of coal. To that end he had plans prepared for a railway line to run from the newly-built East Fife railway to the harbour. The plan shows the line leaving the railway at a point on the boundary of the present nine-hole golf course. It was then to cross the area now occupied by the course, and cut through one of the then unbuilt areas of the town, and from there run along the seafront on an embankment in front of the town to the causeway and so to a coal-loading point somewhere on the quay or the pier.

Fortunately for those who value Elie's traditional character, any wider ambitions that Baird may have had were not realised. His coalfield survey was not very promising, and he would have been persuaded that he would get a better return from investments elsewhere. His Fife coalfields were not developed, he established no foundries or warehouses, and the harbour branch of the railway was never built. If Wood Haven had been enclosed, separated from the new railway line by only one-third of a mile of virtually level ground, Baird might have found the opportunity for development irresistible.

MINOR WORKS

Two minor elements in Baird's harbour works remain to be noted. At some point, most likely when the causeway and the quay had been completed and the traffic in agricultural produce on a substantial scale had resumed, a weighbridge and weigh house were installed on the quay. There appears to be a reference to this small building (which was demolished only a few years ago to clear the site for the Sailing Club's clubhouse) in an Elie Estate Account Book entry for the year 1857-58, which records a payment received of £4 10s rent for "*Part of Granary and New House at Gate*". There would have been a barrier at the weigh house to ensure that all carts had to pass over the weighbridge. The schedule of rates laid down in the Elie Harbour Act of 1857 included a charge of one penny per ton for goods weighed on the harbour weighing machine.

The final improvement - as noted above - came in 1868, when the East Fife Record of 24 January reports "*The new light has been hoisted at the harbour, and to fishermen and others who have occasion to enter this port, its advantages will prove greatly in favour of seamen...*" The light continued to shine through the winter months until 1929.

A HARBOUR-USER'S COMMENTS

An interesting contemporary view of Baird's take-over and development of the harbour is to be found in Henrietta Keddie's account of her family's life at the house of Grange in the middle of the century. Her father, and later her brother Robert, leased and worked the Grange Colliery on Earlsferry Links. Philip Keddie ran the pit from the 1830s to 1852, under recurring difficulties. His son Robert found that the pit had actually been sunk through a seam of valuable ironstone, which his inexpert father had failed to recognise. For some years Robert worked the ironstone and exported it through Elie harbour to iron-smelting furnaces at Newcastle on Tyne. In 1857 it was reported up to three vessels a day were loading with ironstone at Elie. Henrietta's narrative tells what followed the Baird take-over:

"*There was no blast furnace within a long distance for what must be a heavy load of cargo involving heavy carriage of freight. A spend-thrift easy-dealing laird of Elie House ..... successor of young Sir John was long since ruined and in debt. The estate including the harbour on the Firth was sold to of all people one of the great iron masters of Western Scotland. Naturally he did not desire an increase of iron not his own put on the market. He may have wished to recoup himself for the sums of money he had spent on the harbour. The attempted improvements were predicted to be unsatisfactory. Harbour engineering, the most difficult of any, seemed likely to baffle the engineers employed. The currents had not been sufficiently taken into account and the drift of sand increased instead of diminishing threatened to kill the harbour. The apportioning of the harbour dues was in the hands of the new laird and were laid on to such a forbidding extent that when Robert attempted to ship the ore to Newcastle on Tyne furnaces the profit to the leaseholder was next to nil*".

In the Fifeshire Journal of 20 May 1858 there is a report about the shipping of ironstone which shows that Robert tried one last expedient before he was forced to give up. It reads: "*ELIE*

Shipping of Iron Ore at our port, of which we have lately took notice still continues briskly. Only a few days ago two pretty sizeable vessels were cleverly loaded and travelled together for Newcastle. Carts were regularly employed driving ironstone from Grange Colliery at Earlsferry and laid down at our east pier where a large quantity already lies ready for embarkation. The west pier being very unhandy and not at all adapted to the use of carts, owing to the narrowness and inequality of the surface which has long been a grievance among farmers and others who are in the habit of shipping goods here. To obviate the difficulties Mr. Keddie has adopted a novel and at the same time excellent expedient by laying down a temporary narrow railway, on which small carriages are moved quickly by the workmen and it is surprising how soon vessels are loaded and ready for sea by ship by the help of this simple contrivance. As this traffic gives employment to miners, carters and sailors in the locality it is natural for us to wish success to the iron trade".

The Fifeshire Journal's good wishes were of no avail. Whether because of the extra cost of the double-handling of the heavy cargo, or some other factor, Robert's costs became too great. He was forced into bankruptcy and had to return to his profession as a civil engineer. The ironstone mine closed and one source of harbour revenue had gone for ever. The justice of Henrietta's observation that Baird was discriminating against the shipping of ironstone can be shown by one comparison. The 1842 rate for coal at one halfpenny per ton (one penny per ton for strangers) was the same as that for ironstone, not surprisingly for a similar mineral bulk cargo. It was the lowest rate for any bulk cargo. Baird raised the rate for coal to 3 pence per ton and for ironstone to 8 pence. These discriminatory rates were prescribed in his Elie Harbour Act of 1857.

ACCUMULATION OF SAND IN THE HARBOUR

It is apparent from Henrietta's account that the deposition of sand in front of the causeway and in the harbour generally began as soon as the causeway was completed and the wave action and tidal currents that had flowed across the swarf from and perhaps also into Wood Haven were blocked. Her comments on the engineer's design of the harbour presumably reflect the views of her brother, the civil engineer. They were possibly unaware of the way the Admiralty had cut down Moffat's plan, by removing the proposed long breakwater to the west. It seems likely that if that breakwater had been built it would have prevented or at least greatly mitigated the problem of sand deposition, by trapping the sand coming east by longshore drift from the main beach and causing most if not all of it to settle against the breakwater before it could reach the harbour. If that is correct, the sand which now forms the harbour beach and dune, deposited over about 150 years against the 17 foot high causeway wall, would have been deposited instead against the new breakwater and in front of the western part of South Street, and thus formed part of a nearly continuous arc of sandy beach from School Wynd to Chapel Ness.

The accumulation of sand in the harbour has very seriously restricted its capacity. More that half of the 600 foot quay built by Baird has been submerged in the great harbour dune, tapering away to the harbour bed (itself covered in a thick layer of deposited sand) about 250 feet from the root of the pier. It seems possible that before Baird's scheme was carried out the old Swarf Dyke even when intact may not have presented such an effective barrier to the highest waves and tides, and thus allowed some scouring of the harbour; and the old shorter pier would also have had less effect in slowing down the tidal currents in the harbour. The earliest references to sand deposition suggest it resulted from sand being transferred by wave and tide over the Swarf from Wood Haven into the harbour; but this may not have been the real cause of such problems as occurred before Baird's causeway was built. Certainly the deposited sand built up quickly after any possible flow of sand from Wood Haven was completely cut off.

11
Harbour dues and finances

It appears that despite the lapse of 100 years the harbour dues set in 1740 must have remained in force with only a few changes till 1842, when a new Table of Dues was established in the lease which secured the repair of the pier. This table contained 26 separate rates compared with 27 in the 1740 roll; and the order in which the commodities were listed was very nearly the same. It was an up-date, showing relatively few changes in rates.

One important change in 1842 was that the rate for grain (and meal) was increased by about 17% for inhabitants, but actually reduced for strangers, who had formerly had to pay double. The new rates were the same for strangers as for inhabitants, and equalled that set for potatoes in 1740. This was 3/6 per 100 bolls, roughly equivalent to six tons: this remained the rate for potatoes. Equating the rates for strangers and inhabitants for these staple commodities probably reflected the extent of the area from which agricultural produce was drawn as well as the importance of the amount of produce sold to non-resident merchants and millers, some of whom rented space in the granary to receive their cargoes before shipment.

For fish of all kinds the rates for strangers and inhabitants were also made equal; but for most other goods the rates for strangers remained double the inhabitants' rate.

More significant of the great changes that had taken place in farming practice was that the table contained rates for livestock. These were at the same level for strangers as for inhabitants. Such rates must have been in use for a considerable period before 1842, made necessary by the effects of the agricultural revolution which had been gathering momentum in Scotland from the early 18th century. By 1800 great progress, which continued into the 19th century, had been made in the production of all the main crops, combined with the related raising of livestock. Great advances on the supply side were matched by an increase in demand. Increasing family incomes in most parts of Scotland throughout the 18th century led to increased meat consumption. The price of cattle quadrupled over the century, most of the increase taking place after 1740. The fine farmhouses and steadings, many built around the middle of the 19th century, reflect the prosperity of the agriculture that contributed greatly to the export trade of the harbour.

Minor changes made in 1842 were the omission from the later list of specific rates for tar, hemp, taikle, (ship's tackle), pease, malt and kilp (kelp). These were covered in the 1842 Table by a general clause applying the rates for goods of the like kind to any unspecified commodity. Kelp had been a valuable raw material for the chemical and glass industries, being the ash left after burning dried seaweed. It took up to 24 tons of seaweed to produce one ton of kelp, which contained several useful alkaline salts and was worth about £10 to £15. Once other sources of the alkalis became available kelp production declined to extinction, except in the Western Isles where it continued for some time.

The 1842 list continued the 1740 rate for bark, a high one at 6d per ton for inhabitants and 1s. 1½d for strangers. We know from events in the 1830s (noted below) that bark used by tanners was an important import cargo.

In 1857 the harbour dues were again revised, in a Schedule annexed to Baird's Harbour Act. Whereas the 1842 lease specified only 29 separate classes of goods, the 1857 schedule included 139 separate rates. It seems likely that much of this schedule was simply copied from the schedule for some large port, possibly Kirkcaldy or Leith, though almost all the commodities listed are of a kind that might conceivably be landed at or shipped from Elie. For example the charge of 3 pence for the shipping of a barrel bulk (equal to 5 cubic feet) of musical instruments, which at first sight seems an odd entry, might very well be needed. The obvious way to send a piano from Edinburgh to Elie would be to put it on a ship.

The 1857 schedule greatly increased the rates for a variety of goods, notably by completely bringing to an end the long-standing practice of charging inhabitants half the rate charged to strangers. Latterly this had applied largely to manufactured products, and specialised imports, including groceries like dried fruit and pepper. The rates for staple agricultural exports like corn and livestock were actually reduced a little, though the rate for fresh fish was doubled. The rate for coal, as noted above rose to 3d per ton, compared with ½d for inhabitants and 1d for strangers. The rates for other heavy bulk cargoes rose even more. Lime, in 1842 rated like coal, was now charged at 11d per ton, the steepest rise of all. Ironstone, also earlier rated like coal, went up to 8d a ton.

With the exception of the very high charge for ironstone, the new rates were clearly designed to make the harbour attractive to exporters, particularly of agricultural products. Unfortunately, it seems that no detailed harbour accounts survive to show the volumes of the different commodities imported and shipped, or the breakdown of the revenues they generated.

ANCHORAGE DUES

The 1842 lease contained a slightly simpler list of Anchorage Dues (the dues to be paid by vessels entering the harbour) than those set in 1740, listing only 4 classes of vessels instead of 5. The rates were not changed much. The widest class listed in 1740 was "*Ships, Snows, Brigs, Sloops, or other Vessels*" which had to pay 1d. "*for every Nett Tun*", the rate applying to strangers and inhabitants alike. In 1842 "*Steamboats*" were added to this general class, and the rate for inhabitants was reduced to ½d per ton, the rate for strangers remaining at 1d.

Special rates, as in 1740, appear to be intended to encourage the fisheries. "*Drave or Cooper Boats*" were not included in the general class though they were of the appropriate size to belong there. Cooper boats were the boats that followed the herring fishing fleets round the coast to buy and cure their catches. The rates for them were actually lowered from the 1740 rate of 6d per boat for everybody to 2d per boat for inhabitants and 4d for strangers. For yawls and other small fishing boats inhabitants paid 1d, half the 1740 rate, and strangers 2d, the same as in 1740. These payments by fishing boats

appear to be additional to the charge for fish landed at Elie, being one fish in every ten (teind fish), or one in twenty of fish caught by Elie boats and sold elsewhere. It seems most unlikely that the anchorage due of 1d for inhabitants' fishing boats entering the harbour would be exacted on a daily basis from boats that were kept in the harbour, but that some charging system which compounded these dues with the teind fish charge may have existed, though there is no record of this.

The 1857 Act gave powers to William Baird "*to license, appoint and regulate a sufficient Number of Pilots for conducting Vessels into and out of the harbour*" and to fix Pilotage charges within maximum rates specified in the Act. Pilotage was not compulsory, but was at the discretion of the shipmasters. A notice of 1887 records that the licensed pilots were Captain John Gray, harbourmaster, and John Warrender, Fisherman. They had been examined as to their fitness and capacity, and certified as fully qualified by "*Three competent Persons, being Ship Masters well acquainted with the coast*", in this instance three Anstruther ship masters, who are also recorded elsewhere as Commissioners of Anstruther Harbour.

HARBOUR INCOME – DISPUTED DUES

Bald's report declares that the income arising from the harbour and shore dues at the beginning of the century was about £70 or £80 a year, and that if the harbour had been kept in proper repair the income in the late 1840s would have reached several hundred pounds a year. It is clear from the Kilconquhar and Colinsburgh petition in support of Baird's bill that much agricultural produce was directed to other ports because of the poor condition of Elie harbour.

The earliest detailed records date from the 1830s, when the shore master was Philip Wilson, who was paid £5 a year for his trouble. In addition to collecting the dues he was responsible for supervising mooring and berthing, and for keeping an eye on maintenance problems. The total dues he collected clearly did not include the large amounts paid by regular bulk users like David Carstairs the tanner of Colinsburgh, about whose shipments we have some details; and the annual totals as reported varied substantially, perhaps as a result of irregular record-keeping. Wilson reported the following totals for the years from 1831 to 1837:

Year	£	s	d
1831	7	10	4
1832	7	16	8
1832-33	15	13	1
1834	10	4	3
1835	9	18	4
1836	6	16	0
1837	9	15	0

Average per year over 7 years about £10

The average payment made by the tanner over this period (including interest on sums overdue) was nearly £12, which shows the importance of his trade to the harbour. It seems to have contributed between about one-third and one-seventh of the total harbour revenue, depending on which of the estimates you believe.

We have details of the tanner's import shipments for the reason that he was a very determined man prepared to dispute the rates at which he was charged for landing his cargoes. As a consequence the record of his landings and payments has been preserved in the estate papers in the Scottish Record Office. Over the period of 8 years from 1831 to 1838 Carstairs received on average about 30 shipments a year, possibly mainly in ships carrying other cargoes as well, though it seems likely that his shipments of tanbark, which came in large quantities four or five times a year, would represent a complete shipload.

During these 8 years Carstairs imported 1,359 tons of bark, some of which was to supply John Archibald's tannery in Elie. It would benefit both parties to combine their purchasing power and share shipments. He also imported over 10,000 hides, some as part finished leather, and 151 hogsheads of dressing oil. No doubt he also bought hides from local slaughterers. In a letter to Dickson, the estate trustee, he complained that James Luke of Muircambus Mill, the agent to whom all shore dues however collected were remitted, had not treated him fairly. Before Luke became the agent Carstairs had no difficulties over his harbour dues, though he considered the rates were high; but Luke had effectively doubled his charges by exacting the rate for strangers, instead of the inhabitant's rate, as

formerly. For bark, of which such large quantities were imported, this raised the rate from 6 pence to 12 pence per ton (apparently slightly below the rates fixed in 1740). At Leith the rate was 9 pence, which Carstairs said led the Edinburgh tanners to import their bark through Fisherrow at 4 pence per ton. In addition, not all the bark was for his tannery at Colinsburgh: some was for Archibald, who was actually an inhabitant of Elie where his tannery was situated.

The dispute rumbled on, and Carstairs continued to be billed at the strangers' rate. The account mounted up, and was eventually settled by payments in 1838 and 1840 totalling £94 5s 11d, equivalent to around £5000 in current money.

HARBOUR FINANCES

There are records in the estate papers of the total income from and expenditure on the harbour for the years 1842 and 1843, and further details of income, but not expenditure, in William Bald's report, for the years 1844, 1845 and 1846. The information for the later three years comes, according to Bald, from returns made by the lessees under the 1842 lease to the "Tidal Board". The income figures appear to have varied little from year to year:

Year	Income			Expenditure			Net Revenue		
	£	s	d	£	s	d	£	s	d
1842	34	15	0	22	14	10	12	0	2
1843	38	4	9	23	6	1	14	18	8
1844	37	19	2	-			-		
1845	38	9	0	-			-		
1846	36	15	5	-			-		

The figures for the two earlier years suggest that after paying £12 a year in rent to the estate the lessees had very little to show for their capital expenditure on the pier of about £250. On the assumption that the tannery traffic and the shore dues collected by the shoremaster continued at about the same rates in the 1830s it may be that dues paid by other account-holding bulk users amounted in total to about £12 to £16 a year.

Bald reports that Captain Randall believed that the income figures were grossly understated, and had made his own "careful detailed calculation". Captain Randall reckoned the actual total revenue for a single year at £84 8s 4d. The difference must remain unexplained; but Thomas Currie, who took the money and was responsible for reporting the takings for 1844, 1845, and 1846, had the more detailed knowledge but also with a view to a possible future lease had an interest in under-stating the revenue. Captain Randall was a disinterested observer in a position to be well informed about ship movements but must have had less knowledge of the details of the cargoes. Bald also states that an offer had been made "*to pay a rent of £50 per annum for the shore and harbour dues*". This probably refers to the proposals made to the estate in 1839, which offered a guarantee of an annual payment "*equivalent to the average revenue it had received in recent years*".

Some information bearing on harbour revenues comes from the Fife Valuation Rolls of 1857-58 and 1860-61, as recorded in an estate account book.

Subjects	1857 - 1858			1860 - 1861		
	£	s	d	£	s	d
Elie Harbour Dues						
	40	0	0	30	0	0
Elie Fishing						
	10	0	0	10	0	0
Granary Dues (total)						
	43	0	0	45	0	0
Part of Granary and New House at gate						
	4	10	0			
Total						
	97	10	0	85	0	0

These Valuations seem to be based on the revenue principle. The figures do not suggest that after the initial improvement Baird's expensive works attracted a great deal of additional trade to the harbour. Indeed after the pier improvement had been completed the harbour dues apparently fell. The fishing rent was not strictly harbour income, but was paid for the right to conduct stake-net fishing for salmon on the estate's foreshores.

In an estate account book containing a record of cash paid and cash received a payment is recorded under the heading "Harbour" in October 1857 of £6 2s 6d to R Pousty, being £6 for 15 weeks wages and 2s 6d for some unspecified extra service. This is the only payment recorded in respect of the harbour, and possibly indicates that by this date

the harbourmaster was being paid about £21 a year, a steep rise from the £5 paid to Philip Wilson in the 1830s.

In the same account book there is an analysis under 9 broad heads, of which "Harbour" is one, of estate income for the year ended 31 May 1861. The harbour income is detailed month by month, but not further broken down. The total for the year is £107 9s 5d, with the monthly figures ranging from a low of under £4 in December to a high of nearly £20 in May. This total compares with the Valuation Roll figures for the same year of £30 for harbour dues or £85 including granary dues and fishing rents.

GRANARY FINANCES

The estate papers in the Scottish Record Office contain several financial records which are the short sections that happen to have survived of what were presumably once continuous records which covered a much longer period. One of these fragments, headed "*Dr. Robert Maltman in account with Mr. Robert Carstairs*" contains detailed accounts relating to the granary. These cover the period 22 November 1814 to 12 December 1815, and show rents received totalling £74 13s 1½d and expenses paid totalling £21 16s 9d. The net balance of £52 16s 4½d was recorded as "*Remains to be divided*". One third of that sum was paid by Maltman to Robert Carstairs who acted for the proprietor of the estate.

The heading indicates that Maltman had the financial management of the granary. A concluding entry records his acknowledgement that he himself had received one third of the "Remains". Presumably there once was a comparable account between Maltman and a third party who received the remaining third; but this would not be part of the estate papers. It may be deduced that Maltman and the third party had outstanding loans secured over the granary, and that Colonel Robert Anstruther's rights over the granary had by this date been acquired by the estate. The granary was certainly part of the estate that William Baird bought in 1853.

12
The last decades of the century

Pier repairs of 1880

It appears from the record of substantial repair work carried out in 1880 that at the outer end of the then 20-year old pier the foundations of the north-east corner had begun to give way and the subsiding masonry above had suffered severe damage. That corner, unlike the north-west corner, was not buttressed by the broad end of the pier against the heavy pressures of storm waves coming from the west.

The remedial work required the taking down of the corner and a considerable length of piling, including sheet piling, to form a coffer-dam to allow the excavation of over 220 cubic yards of the sea-bed and the placing of 163 cubic yards of concrete foundations and 400 cubic yards of clay. The projecting bank of clay which is visible at low water springs around the base of the end of the pier was presumably put in place to buttress the base as part of the remedial work at this time. It would reinforce and protect the main clay base which had been laid when the pier was built to provide a secure foundation for its outer end, replacing the sand above the underlying rock. Around the corner the damaged stonework had to be re-built on the new foundations and some additional ashlar blocks were required. The contract documents show that the "paal" (bollard) nearest the corner and the adjacent steps had to be re-set. With this major repair the pier work of the 1850s has stood the test of time very well, though there is evidence of some subsidence in the level of the parapet wall close to its outer end.

A draft contract for this repair contains a price of £606 15s 5d: Honeyman and Dean, the contractors, of Musselburgh and Ladybank, submitted a bill of £768 18s 5d in December 1880: their final account of September 1881, agreed after much dispute about extras, and the bankrupting of their Ladybank subsidiary, reduced the total to £618 3s 5d. William Baird and his factor Allan Jamieson were not to be trifled with.

The Mars boys

In the 1880s the granary began to be used each year in the summer, after the potato traffic had come to an end, to provide holiday quarters for boys from an Edinburgh reformatory. The East Fife Record of 3 July 1881 reported "*At the granary a number of women are busily engaged in washing out and cleaning the floors to accommodate the Blackfriars Industrial School, who to the number of about 180 are, as in former seasons, to arrive for a three week stay*". A small extension, shown in the photograph (2) had been built on to the south-west corner of the granary to provide a cookhouse for these visitors. In later years boys from the United Industrial School in Edinburgh and boys from the Mars Training Ship moored in the Tay opposite Dundee came each summer to the granary for the same purpose. In the collective memory of Elie all these holiday visitors are remembered as "*the Mars boys*", marching, after their arrival by train, in proper regimental fashion from the station to the granary. Their morning ablutions took the form of a daily "*dook*" off the end of the pier. Even those who could not swim could get into the water by the pierhead steps. The Mars boys had their last holiday at Elie in 1929.

Reduction of harbour dues 1884

While the summer excursion cruises were bringing big increases in passenger traffic the cargo trade was obviously in decline. In an attempt to attract more traffic, and perhaps to compete with the now well-established railway and possibly also nearby harbours offering lower rates, the proprietor published in 1884 "*Reduced Schedules of the Rates and Duties to be levied until further orders at Elie Harbour.*"

The categories of charges and the commodities listed repeat in virtually identical terms the lists in the Schedules laid down in the 1857 Act, except for two significant omissions. In 1857 there had been special low rates for "*All Boats entirely open, landing or taking on board goods or dried or* salted fish" and "*All drave or large Boats entering the harbour or Precincts thereof with fresh fish*". By 1884 the other harbours of the East Neuk had come to dominate the fishing industry, and stranger boats would enter Elie only to seek refuge from storms, though there were still local boats engaged in fishing. The other omission was of rates for craneage. This suggests that developments in cargo-handling by ships of the kind that frequented Elie at this period had made the use of harbour cranes unnecessary. In the absence of detailed accounts of harbour revenues it is not possible to say whether the harbour actually had its own cranes earlier in the century.

The goods for which rates were materially reduced, usually by a third but sometimes by a half or more, appear to be those which would make up the bulk of the harbour's traffic. They were mostly agricultural products or fish, or commodities or goods used in agriculture or fishing, and the raw materials of local industries and trades, including building, ship-building, brewing, tanning, and blacksmith work. For most consumer goods the rates remained unchanged, with the exception of "*Groceries, viz. Almonds, Figs, Cinnamon, Currants, Pepper, Pimento, Plums, Prunes, raisins, and the like*," for which the rate was lowered from 3d per barrel bulk to 1d. The rate on sugar was also reduced, but not by so much, from 1s 4d to 10d per ton. For these commodities 8 barrels bulk was considered equivalent to a ton.

It does not appear that anyone detected that the new schedules included two unlawful charges. The 1857 Act prescribed the maximum rates that might be charged. The 1857 rate was limited to ½d each for pigs, and this was raised illegally to 1d. For scythe stones, a vital piece of the harvester's kit, the 1857 rate was 1d per score, raised in 1884 to 2d per score. The 1884 charges remained in force until 1955, though less and less used as the cargo traffic declined to complete extinction about 1930.

FISHING IN THE 1880s

In addition to the cargo and passenger traffic, the latter at this date being almost entirely excursion passengers, there was a substantial amount of fishing activity. By the 1880s, in a Guide to the East Neuk of Fife which gives a detailed account of Elie, it is reported that "*The harbour of Elie now serves for Earlsferry as well, and yet there are only twelve fishing boats, with twenty men and boys.*" Elie was not one of the main fishing-harbours of the East Neuk, but it appears fishing provided a livelihood for about twelve families, apart from probably one or two more who rented and worked the stake-net fishing on the foreshore of the Elie estate. The two small harbours of Earlsferry also continued to be used by fishermen, contrary to the report in the Guide.

THE POTATO TRADE

Though there were other agricultural exports, notably grain and livestock, the newspaper reports for the later part of the century focus chiefly on potatoes. It seems likely that the higher-value products, particularly livestock, would increasingly be sent by rail. The railway provided loading points much closer to the farms than Elie harbour; and for the livestock trade easier access and shorter journey times were material advantages.

The potato trade was naturally markedly seasonal. The reports indicate that it usually began in November, after the lifting of the main crop, and went on until May. The "potato boats" (14) were regular visitors to the harbour over this six-month period, being small sailing vessels variously recorded as smacks, schooners, ketches and brigs. The illustration (23) showing a brig (or possibly its variant cousin the brigantine - the disorder of the rigging of the mizzen mast makes identification doubtful) aground near Kincraig, gives a good impression of a ship type that would have been familiar in Elie harbour for many years, and was to continue in use into the 20th century.

Few of these little ships would carry much more than 100 tons or so, but there were plenty of them. A typical report in the East Fife Record of 27 November, 1885 reads "*Potato shipping. This trade had again begun at the harbour. Two vessels have already left for English ports, viz. the smacks Peace and Plenty and Marmaduke. The former was loaded by Mr. Buttercase and the latter by Mr. Bell.*" The smaller of the two potato boats shown in the illustration is the same size as the larger Fifies and Zulus of the fishing fleet.

From other reports it appears that Mr. Bell was the farmer of Stenton, near St. Monance, and that Mr. Buttercase was probably a farmer, near Largo. What role the merchants who rented space in the granary played in these shipments is not clear. Their

14. Potato boats at the pier - 1882

15. Paddle steamer at Galloway jetty c.1891

16. Paddle steamer at Galloway jetty c.1895

17. Cannon on the Law - early 20th century

main supplies may have come from smaller farms than those of Mr. Buttercase and Mr. Bell.

Other ships named in the reports are the *Rose in June*, and the *Spray*, both described as regular visitors, the *Two Friends*, the *Walker* of Dundee (which sailed for Southampton), the *Seabird*, the *Daker* and the *Whim*.

Other reports show that the harbour of St. Monans was also used for the potato trade. It would be very convenient for Mr. Bell of Stenton; but the fishermen of St. Monans would have the prior claim on harbour space there, particularly during the winter herring fishing season. The East Fife Record of 11 January 1901 records *"On Saturday the sketch (sic) Hazard, of Guernsey, arrived from Tayport to load potatoes. She was chartered for St. Monans, but owing to the crowded state of the harbour she could not get in there, and after waiting several hours the Hazard bore up for Elie. The Spartan sailed on Monday evening last."*

Another report, from 1886, shows the landing at Elie of a rather surprising cargo, presumably reflecting the value of a paying cargo to a ship coming north to load potatoes. *"The Two Friends, after discharging English coals, left on Thursday for St. Monance to load potatoes."*

THE GALLOWAY COMPANY – A STEAMER PIER

Excursion cruising had gone from strength to strength, with the development of fine paddle steamers built for the purpose. By the late 1880s the Galloway Saloon Steam Packet Company had become the only company offering regular cruises on the Forth. The Company opened negotiations with Mr. William Baird, who had succeeded to the estate on his father's death in 1864, to build a jetty suitable for paddle steamers at the harbour. It took some time for the parties to come to an agreement. To make the new pier accessible at all states of tide it would have to be outside the existing pier. The site chosen was the one on the north-west side of the Apple Rock that had been identified by the Stevensons in 1836 as one of the two sites they then proposed for cargo wharves. In June 1886, perhaps in an attempt to put pressure on Baird, the Company obtained agreement in principle from Earlsferry Town Council to build a low-water pier at Earlsferry. They eventually reached agreement

with Baird early in 1888, to build a jetty on their chosen site.

The structure was of piles driven into the sand, and, where necessary, anchored to the bare rock by concrete. The deck was wooden staging capable of being removed in winter, when the Galloway Company laid up its cruising fleet, to reduce the risk of storm damage. A concrete pathway across the very rough but level surface of the Apple Rock was laid to connect the bridge from the deck to the roadway at the granary. All the work was completed and brought into use in 1889. A few remains of the structure and the pathway are still to be seen.

The photographs (15,16) show two different steamers at the jetty, and the sketch (19) shows its structure as seen from an approaching vessel. The *Wemyss Castle*, built in 1872 is in the one that displays the structure of the landing stage and its connecting bridge. The other photograph shows one of the later ships, with much better saloon accommodation for passengers, possibly the *Edinburgh Castle*. The larger Galloway steamers like the *Edinburgh Castle* could reach the speed of 15 knots, and carry 700 to 800 passengers; and their state-of-the-art fittings contributed to their considerable success in attracting business.

In the winter of 1889, following damage to paddles caused by projecting rocks, an additional row of piles was driven to enable the steamers to be more securely and safely moored. Two years later additional struts and braces were added to stiffen the structure and some rocks and displaced concrete removed by blasting. With these improvements the pier continued in use until the 1920s.

In addition to their cruising services the Galloway Company made an attempt in the late 1880s to establish commuter services to Edinburgh from Largo and Elie. This service enabled business men and others to stay in Elie with their holidaying families, while continuing to earn their daily bread in Edinburgh. To achieve the fastest possible service for these summer commuters the company went so far in 1889 as to provide a separate steamer for each resort.

Since the steamers of the period could make the crossing from pier to pier in about an hour this was perfectly practicable, so practicable and effective that the North British Railway Company (the NBR as it was usually known) complained about the interference with its traffic. This was not surprising, as the railway connection to Edinburgh took much longer because it depended at that time on the rail-ferry service between Granton and Burntisland. (The Forth Bridge was not opened until 1890).

By this period the NBR had come to own a substantial proportion of the Galloway Company shares. The clash of interests led to negotiations in which the NBR acquired a majority interest in the steamer company. Thereafter there was no prospect that the steamers would compete seriously with the railway for commuter or other ordinary passenger traffic. Excursion cruises were another matter, and here the NBR continued the ambitious policies of the Galloway Company, in a field of which they had considerable experience because of the services they ran on the Clyde and also on Loch Lomond.

A DISPUTE ABOUT LANDING CHARGES

The increasing passenger landings (on a single trip in May 1891 the *Tantallon Castle* landed 220 passengers) which followed the development of services made possible by the new all-tide pier led to a dispute between the Galloway Company and the estate. The proprietor had thought to add to the harbour's income by making a landing charge for every passenger, as was done at many other piers in Scotland. Since 1890 the Galloway Company had been running cruises which called twice at Elie, which permitted passengers to spend an afternoon ashore.

The schedule of charges issued in 1884 had included no charges for landing passengers. In this it followed the list of dues prescribed in the 1842 lease, and Sir John Anstruther's Ordinance of 1740. There was likewise no provision in William Scott's Royal Charter of 1601 for charging landing fees, although there was a provision that incoming ships were charged the round sum of eightpence (after 1603 the equivalent of two-thirds of a penny sterling) for "the skipper and marines."

The Company had two substantial arguments for refusing to pay passenger landing charges. First, the 1857 Act governing the management of the harbour contained no power to charge such fees; and, second, the Company had itself built, by agreement with the estate, the pier on which the passengers landed and the pathway which led them to a roadway open to the public at no charge. In the event, the proprietor dropped the proposal.

ELIE IN 1891

In October 1891 the East Fife Record reported that this had been an exceptionally good season for the whole Fifeshire coast. "*Elie has maintained her lead as the most attractive and picturesque resort on either side of the Forth*." For a number of years around this period the newspapers record great building activity at Elie, much of it providing houses mainly used as holiday homes, most of them rented for the purpose. A lyrical description of developments at this time is to be found in a newspaper report recorded in "The Shores of Fife", a rather unusual little guide book to have been produced during the severe paper rationing of World War II. "*But it is in comparatively recent years that Earlsferry and Elie have broken from the rough old chrysalis of a trading and fishing town, and have become, in the summer season, butterflies of fashion*".

The proprietor of the harbour contributed his share to maintaining Elie's attractions. Mr. Baird had the flagstaff on the Law re-furbished, and the cannons there "*mounted on new carriages, the muzzles pointing seaward*." It seems very likely that Baird had installed these cannons, which were no doubt obsolete and purely ornamental. Old cannons were a valuable source of high-quality scrap-iron and the iron-founder would be able to choose some handsome examples to display. He had placed three seats on the Law, and had retaining walls built to prevent landslips, making the Law "*a neat and tasteful place of resort*" and "*a pleasant lounge for the summer visitors*." The illustration (17) shows one of the cannon, perhaps with its new carriage, also the weigh-house, three fishing boats drawn up above Lucky's Hole, and salmon stake nets drying on their poles on the dune. The illustration (18) showing salmon nets in greater detail suggests that the seawall protecting the Toft seagardens had not been completed at this period, though the photograph may be of an earlier date.

CRUISING IN THE 1890s

The 1890s were the high period of summer cruising on the Forth. The principal ship for the daily cruises which called at Elie and North Berwick en route to round the Bass Rock or the May Island, or sometimes the Bell Rock, was the second *Tantallon Castle*. She was 240 tons, built in 1887 at Leith, and lengthened from 190 feet to 202 feet in 1895. On the Elie run she replaced the smaller and slower *Edinburgh Castle*, which was transferred to service mainly in the upper estuary. The Galloway schedules show that the *Tantallon Castle*, with the slightly smaller *Stirling Castle*, was making two calls at Elie every day allowing visitors a considerable period ashore.

With their other ships serving the upper estuary on regular runs that took in a number of harbours from Aberdour to Stirling, the Galloway Company ran six fine steamers on the Forth. All of them were in service until May 1898, when the *Tantallon Castle* and the *Stirling Castle* were sold to Turkish owners on the Bosphorus, and two other ships were scrapped. However, regular services to Elie were restored in 1899, with the building of replacements for the *Tantallon* and *Stirling Castles*. The illustration (19) shows the new *Tantallon Castle*, at 210 feet and 393 tons the largest vessel ever to use the Apple Rock pier, in Cardiff Docks after her sale to Hawthorn Bros. of London in 1901. She had been the Company's flagship for only two years. The 1900 cruising schedules were similar to those of 1897.

PROMENADE PROJECT OF 1899

In 1899 William Baird had a plan prepared by the Edinburgh Civil Engineers Belfrage and Carfrae for a new promenade at Wood Haven. It was to be formed by building an embankment behind a sea-wall on the foreshore. The sea-wall was to run in a straight line from the shoreward end of the harbour causeway to the Mid-rock of Wood Haven, which projects from the shore dunes about 220 yards to the east. The sea-wall, founded deep below the sand and shingle of the beach, was to rise about 9 feet above beach level. The promenade was to have a 6 foot pavement immediately behind a 3 foot high parapet, and a 24 foot roadway behind. Appropriate in-fill materials were specified to fill the gaps between the straight roadway and the curving shoreline in front of Braehead Cottage, the Coastguard Station and the dune between the Coastguard site and the Mid-rock. There can be little doubt that the purpose of this project was to improve the attractions of Elie as a resort, and perhaps also to make possible the building of further villas on the seafront above Wood Haven.

The plans were fully detailed, and tender documents were prepared inviting offers by 22 July. It was a condition that the work should be completed by 22 November, subject to a penalty of 10 shillings for every day's delay after that date. In the meantime, however, the Admiralty had had to be consulted, and their reply to the estate factor was unhelpful. Their letter said that the advantages to the Admiralty of the proposed road (these are not described in the letter, but the obvious one was the direct access from the harbour to the Coastguard Station by a much better road than the narrow Admiralty Lane) would not be sufficient to warrant the extra expense of building the new boundary wall that would be needed to enclose the Coastguard site. The letter concluded by asking what action the proprietor now proposed to take.

A subsequent reminder from the Admiralty seeking a reply rather suggests that they hoped the proprietor would offer to bear or contribute to the costs of the wall to enable his scheme to proceed. If so, they were to be disappointed, for in the event the proprietor simply abandoned the ambitious scheme. He had not been able to persuade the proprietor of an essential strip of land adjoining the landward end of the causeway to sell it for the building of the new promenade. A clue to the sea defence that took its place is to be found in part of the specification for the scheme which includes an item *"Allow for removing existing sleeper wall and laying material aside for proprietor."*

Subsequent correspondence shows that, after the project was abandoned, the engineers specified and supervised a lesser scheme which appears to have been little more than repairing and perhaps extending the old sleeper wall. The correspondence shows that one of the main problems with this wall was that the sea had removed much of its back-filling. The repair work included putting in stone filling behind the wall and bracing it from behind with "counter-forts", presumably substantial buried buttresses. The engineers put the estate to extra expense by specifying some of this work about which they had not informed the factor, and had to explain themselves before the contractor was paid. This smaller work was completed by 22 November, the date originally set for the completion of the project as first planned. The abandonment of the larger scheme ended the estate's plans for the further development of Elie harbour.

13

The harbour before August 1914

SHIPPING IN THE EARLY 20TH CENTURY

At the beginning of the century the harbour was in active use for the shipping of agricultural produce mainly, if not by this date exclusively potatoes. Coal and ironstone exports from Elie had come to an end. Summer excursion cruises provided most of the traffic at this period. These cruises were also useful to some Edinburgh people, as a convenient way to make the journey for holiday visits.

In 1901 the Galloway Company had only one vessel cruising in the outer firth, the new *Stirling Castle*, which made regular calls at Elie throughout the summer. She was replaced in 1906 by the *Roslin Castle*, a new screw steamer of 392 tons and 185 feet long. The illustration (20) shows the *Roslin Castle* approaching the pier.

In 1908, after the sale of the *Roslin Castle* in March to the Admiralty - she became *HMS Nimble* - there were no cruises in the outer firth. In 1909 calls at Elie were resumed with the *Redgauntlet*, built in 1895 and originally used by the NBR on the Clyde. She had the same engine power as the *Roslin Castle*, but was longer and less beamy, and a much lighter ship, being only 277 tons. Her fine lines and lighter displacement made her appreciably faster, which improved the service she could deliver. Elie had calls every Monday, Tuesday, Thursday and Friday, and two calls allowing a good period ashore on Saturday. Excursion cruises continued on this pattern until 2 August 1914, when they were prohibited by the Admiralty, just before the outbreak of World War I. In 1916 the *Redgauntlet* went off to be a minesweeper.

A SEWER IN THE CAUSEWAY

As part of the drainage scheme they were carrying out in 1905 the Town Council needed Mr. Baird's approval to dig a trench in the harbour road for a sewer. The laird agreed this might be done at no charge, provided there was no interference with his right to dig up the road as he might determine to help clear sand out of the harbour. The notion of opening a sluice tunnel or tunnels through

the causeway has since been mooted on several occasions, but never taken up, though as later noted sluices were opened through the pier. The harbour beach has now become such a valued amenity that it seems unlikely that sluices will ever be put in place that might take some of it away.

ELIE YACHT CLUB

The records of the Elie Yacht Club do not seem to have survived, but press reports show that it was active in the first decade of the century. The account of a regatta on Monday 21 August 1905 shows that the club was quite small. The regatta had been postponed from the Saturday before; we can deduce this was because the weather was so fine that there was no wind, since on that day lifeboat collecting tins were busy at the harbour. There was also a demonstration that afternoon by the Coastguards of rescue work using a breeches buoy from the pier, and of the resuscitation of someone apparently drowned.

On the Monday the postponed races were run from the Commodore's yacht, anchored in the bay to mark one end of the start line. The photograph (21) shows a yacht of the period, a gaff-rigged cutter of perhaps 40 feet or more, sailing in the bay. There were three sailing races, one for yawls with 4 entries, one for yachts with 3 entries, and one for small boats racing under a handicap system with fixed time allowances, for which there were 4 entries. For yawls and yachts the race was over a three-mile course, while the small boats had a two-mile course. A race for rowing boats from the harbour to the Thill Rock buoy and back was won by the coastguard crew. A similar regatta is reported in 1909, and it seems possible that these were annual events. The Club was disbanded in 1911, when the Commodore's cannon was presented to the Town Council.

ELIE NESS LIGHTHOUSE

It was not until 1908 that a navigation light began to flash from a lighthouse on Elie Ness, and then only

18. Salmon nets drying - early 20th century

19. The Tantallon Castle of 1899

20. Roslin Castle approaching Elie

21. Edwardian yacht in Elie Bay

22. Hydroplanes at harbour beach - 1913

23. Wreck of brig near Kincraig - 1912

24. Wreck of the Totleben off Chapel Ness - 1912

25. Attempted salvage of the Totleben - 1912

after a good deal of pressure from Master Mariners frequenting the Forth. Their main argument was that in dirty weather when off Elie Ness, (which they describe as a decided projection towards the shipping channel from the north shore of the Forth) they could not see the lights on the Isle of May and Inchkeith, the two navigation aids for this passage. The Commissioner's Engineer, David Stevenson, considered the case was well established. In 1907, the President of the Board of Trade, David Lloyd George, who was the Chairman of a supervisory board for lighthouses throughout the United Kingdom, gave his approval.

It was arranged that HM Coastguards at Elie should attend the light, which was to be fuelled by acetylene gas. The building work began at the end of 1907, and a Notice to Mariners was duly issued that a flashing white light would be exhibited from an unwatched Beacon Light on Elie Ness from 1st October 1908. The acetylene system was replaced by electricity supplied from the mains in 1959. With aids like radar and Global Monitoring systems lighthouses are no longer the vital aids they were for commercial shipping, but they are still useful and valued particularly by small boat users.

A minor change had been made in the local navigation light system in 1905, when the estate asked the Northern Lighthouse Board for permission to change the colour of the pierhead light from white to red, probably to distinguish it from the bright lights in the town behind. The Board decided that a change in colour should be authorised, but that it would have to be from white to green. This was the correct colour to show on the starboard hand for vessels sailing past Elie to go on up the Forth as well as for vessels entering Elie Harbour.

HYDROPLANES AT THE HARBOUR

The residents of Elie must have been very surprised one day near the end of September 1913, when two seaplanes (referred to in the press of the period as *"hydroplanes"*) landed at Elie Harbour, and were hauled up above high water on the dune beside the causeway. (22) Perhaps some aviation pioneer was providing a home demonstration, hoping to persuade Mr. Baird to invest in the infant industry, or perhaps Mr. Baird was already investing in this promising new technology. The planes remained at the harbour from Wednesday till Saturday, *"their departure being witnessed by a large crowd of spectators."* It was only about 90 years since the first steamships had been seen at the harbour

TWO WRECKS

Over the centuries there have been many wrecks in Elie bay and on the nearby coast, too many to record in this account of the harbour. One wreck which shows how small sailing ships continued to ply their trade on the Forth estuary well into the 20th century is shown in the illustration (23). This is from a postcard of 1912 which shows a wreck which may have taken place in that year or perhaps a year or so earlier, of a brig (or brigantine) ashore near Kincraig. Members of the crew can be seen in the stern, under a tangled mess of the rigging of the mizzen mast. This small ship is typical of the many such ships which frequented Elie Harbour in earlier years.

Also in 1912 there was a notable wreck which caused much activity at the harbour over a fair period. On February 20 1912 the *Graf-Totleben* of Riga, having loaded coal at Methil, sailed too close along the shore and attempted to pass between the East Vows and Chapel Ness. She ran aground on the Inner Vows, the outermost of the line of rocks that stretches from Chapel Ness towards the east Vows. The crew were all rescued, possibly by breeches-buoy.

The 1500-ton ship had been built at Renfrew for Norwegian owners in 1881. After her sale to a Russian company her name was changed from *Skjold* to *Graf-Totleben*, honouring Count Ivanovich Totleben, a famous 19th century Russian general and military engineer.

The ship was partly unloaded, pulled off the rocks and towed across the bay to lie on the sand outside the harbour near the pier so that the rest of her cargo could be unloaded. The illustration (24) shows the ship aground on the Inner Vows. In the foreground the cable and bucket gear used to unload some of the cargo can be seen, possibly on the site from which a breeches-buoy had been used by the Coastguard rescue team to save the crew.

The illustration (25) shows the ship lying aground outside the harbour, with part of her coal cargo in a heap deposited on the pier, having been transferred there by the large fishing boat with a

Kirkcaldy registration. The fishing-boat's derrick, powered by a horse on the pier, is being used to empty the fish-hold of its load of coal. Despite the unloading the *Graf-Totleben* proved to be so severely damaged as to become a total loss.

SAND PROBLEMS - SLUICES THROUGH THE PIER

Over the years after the major works of the 1850s the effect of the new structures upon the tidal currents in the bay caused large amounts of sand to be deposited in the area of foreshore enclosed by the Toft, the causeway, the quay and the pier. In earlier centuries some effect of this sort must have been observed after the building of the Swarf Dyke, the quay and the pier around 1600; but these works probably did not affect the tidal currents quite as much as the later larger structures. The original pier was considerably shorter; and the Swarf Dyke may have been overflowed at the highest tides for much of its lifetime.

At all events, in the later decades of the 19th century the rate at which sand accumulated in the harbour increased greatly, ultimately creating the harbour beach with its dune behind, which completely buried the western wall of the causeway. Deposited sand covered much of the harbour bed, greatly reducing the length of William Baird's quay. As the sand accumulated and the water shallowed, the tidal currents would be further slowed and the rate of deposition probably increased. Early in the 20th century the effective area of the harbour had been so reduced that the proprietor had to take action or see his harbour become almost useless.

A report was prepared in 1912 by the Stevensons, the long-established marine civil engineers, on the problem of sand accumulating against the pier, with the recommendation that two culverts should be driven through it to allow tide and wave-generated currents to scour the sand from the inner face of the pier and the harbour bed nearby. Plans were drawn up to implement their recommendations. These bear the name of the equally well-known Robert McAlpine and Sons, the engineering contractors.

The culverts, later always referred to as sluices, were 4 feet in width by 5 feet in height and were lined with concrete 2 feet thick for the walls, 18 inches thick for the roofs, and six inches thick for the floors. 600 tons of accumulated sand had to be removed to permit the driving of the sluices through the base of the pier.

In their tender of 23 August 1912 McAlpines offered to carry out the work, including the provision of greenheart booms at the outer ends of the sluices to permit them to be closed in stormy weather, for the sum of £575. This was on the understanding that work would start at once, obviously to take advantage of favourable weather conditions before the usual autumn storms. The tender letter shows that at that period cargoes were still being loaded and unloaded from the pier, as McAlpines stipulated that the pier would require to be closed to cart traffic.

The scheme proved successful though its effect was, not surprisingly, limited. It kept the area close to the pier relatively free of sand, but had progressively less effect over the harbour bed further from the pier. Close to the pier the sand does not rise above the base of the sluice openings; but even there the sand is well above the harbour bed.

At times it appears the deposit may be 5 feet deep and more further from the pier over much of the harbour bed below. In 1710 the historian Sibbald recorded that the harbour provided 22 feet of water at spring tides. The 1600 pier was significantly higher than the present pier, and Sibbald may have simply measured the height of the pier above the harbour bed. The deck of the pier is now about 15 feet above the sand. The formation of the sluices was the last improvement the harbour was to see for a long time. The First World War was to bring great changes, and the harbour was to lose most of its traffic within less than 20 years.

26. Crew of Elie Radio Signal Station - 1914

27. WWII machine-gun emplacement at Chapel Ness

28. Harbour mooring pattern - 1944

29. Provider II c.1980

14

The First World War and its sequel

EFFECTS ON THE EAST NEUK

In August 1914 the East Fife Observer reviewed the effects of the outbreak of war on the communities of the East Neuk. About the Elie area it had this to say *"Not relying on fishing, the twin burghs of Elie and Earlsferry were not so adversely affected by the war as the neighbouring communities."* The Observer reported that many summer visitors stayed on longer in both burghs. The steamer services were suspended in August, but visitors continued to come by train. One measure that affected all those whose houses faced the sea was that their house lights had to be *"dwarfed"*.

More importantly for all the shipping on the Forth, all the navigation lights on the lighthouses in the firth were initially extinguished. Later a control regime was established which provided for reduced-power lights to be shown at the May and other lighthouses when required, mainly for naval purposes. So-called "secret" lights were also installed at three sites, including Elie Ness Lighthouse, to assist naval craft in their anti-submarine patrols. It seems likely that the light on Elie pier would be extinguished also. The Thill Rock buoy was removed for the duration.

The suspension of the steamer services, which were not restored till some time after the war, took away most of Elie Harbour's traffic. It seems unlikely, however, that the seasonal trade in the shipping of potatoes would have had to be suspended.

DEFENCE MEASURES - THE FIDRA BOOM

Measures for the defence of the naval base at Rosyth had very serious consequences for the fishing communities. The laying of minefields in the Forth and the operations of naval patrols, particularly night operations, led to severe restrictions on fishing, greatly affected also by the commandeering of boats. In 1915, from Anstruther alone, 22 drifters were commandeered for naval use.

U-boats were active in the Forth area from the beginning of the war, and the anti-submarine defences in the area were repeatedly improved. In 1916 they required particular strengthening when an anchorage for the Grand Fleet was created east of the Forth Bridge. Ron Morris records in *Aboard HMS May Island* that *"An anti-submarine boom was laid between the island of Fidra off the Lothian coast and Elie on the Fife coast, and two lines of hydrophones operated from shore stations on Fidra and at Elie were laid across the seabed to the seaward of the boom."* Later, in 1917, further hydrophone lines were laid from Crail and from Seacliffe in East Lothian. The hydrophone system had been developed at the Admiralty Experimental Station at Hawkcraig, near Aberdour.

The boom, known as the Fidra boom, consisted of large steel floats supporting heavy steel nets designed to be impenetrable by submarines. Between the two long sections extending from each shore, there was a two mile gap closed by "indicator nets", sections of which were controlled by boom defence vessels and could be opened or closed to meet operational requirements.

On the Fife side the boom ended at Elie Ness, where the hydrophone listening station and its crew were housed in the *"hydrophone huts"* built close to Elie Lighthouse. A wireless station, initially manned by the Coastguard Service, had earlier been established on the same site. The station had a crew of naval ratings and one civilian, commanded by a Chief Petty Officer (26). It had satellite stations at Anstruther and on the Isle of May. Despite its convenient location, the tidal and very basic harbour of Elie could play little if any part in the servicing and maintenance of the boom, which had been constructed at Methil, where the docks with all their engineering and other facilities were well placed to undertake the work. No doubt naval craft would have occasion to call at Elie from time to time. There is no evidence at the harbour that any work was ever carried out there to adapt it for any naval purpose.

THE END OF EXCURSION CRUISING

By 1919 the Galloway piers on the Forth had been neglected for a number of years. In common with the other Galloway installations, the pier at Elie and its associated ticket booth were in poor condition. The NBR decided not to restart their Forth cruising services, which meant a serious loss of income for the harbour. Because there were good passenger train services from Edinburgh and Glasgow the holiday trade of Elie and Earlsferry (which had continued by train all through the war) was not so seriously affected, except for the loss of custom for shops and catering establishments from the crowds of day trippers from the excursion steamers, which had often delivered several hundred passengers at a time. The cargo trade continued for a number of years, now almost exclusively in potatoes. It was seasonal and did not produce much revenue.

July 19, 1919, was declared to be Peace Day, and there were national celebrations, hopefully marking the end of the great wars. The Elie festivities included a bonfire and a fireworks display at the harbour, provided by Captain Baird who had succeeded to the estate.

In 1922 Kirk Deas and Company of Leith restarted Forth cruises, occasionally offering long day cruises to the outer firth, which included time ashore at Elie, using the decayed but still just serviceable Galloway pier. The service was provided by the Conqueror, (131 feet and 199 tons), a powerful ex-tug; but it did not last long. She was bought by the Stanley-Butler Steamship Company of Kirkcaldy, which continued the Elie service in 1924; but in 1925 the Conqueror was given a restricted licence which did not permit cruising in the outer firth. This marked the end of Elie as a regular cruise destination.

For almost 50 years, with a break of 8 years caused by the First World War, excursion steamers had enlivened the summer scene at Elie Harbour, and brought tens of thousands of visitors to the town. The end of the excursion services marked a further decline in the fortunes of the harbour, which for a number of years was not to be a very active place.

There was a flicker of renewed interest in 1929, when an approach was made to the Town Council by one company still running services on the upper Forth. They asked if the Council would repair the disintegrating steamer pier. Nothing came of this, not surprisingly, since the Council did not own the harbour and it was actually outside the burgh boundary at that date. The pier fell into complete disrepair. By the mid 1930s most of the remains had been cleared away, although a few traces are still to be seen.

THE LAST CARGOES

The ending of the harbour's last commercial use, a few small fishing boats excepted, was not long in coming. From the later part of the 19th century the harbour had been steadily losing its agricultural export trade, and what little import trade it retained, to the railway. In addition to the line around the Fife coast the North British Railway (later the London and North Eastern Railway) operated a goods line a few miles inland, called the Lochty Siding, which was designed to serve a wide farming area, as well as some coal mines. It is not surprising that the railway took more and more of the agricultural traffic. For the farmer driving his produce by horse and cart, and his livestock on their own legs, a short distance to the loading point was a great advantage.

What is surprising is that the shipping of potatoes from Elie continued, though on a reduced scale, until about 1930. These cargoes would come from the farms in easy reach of the harbour, following long-established practice and taking advantage of the low rates charged by the cheaply-run small sailing ships of the coastal trade (14, 23), carrying cargoes for which speedy delivery was not important. However, this form of transport was coming to the end of its very long life, with the notable exception of the Thames barges, operating in the very special circumstances, not paralleled anywhere in Scotland, of the trade between their estuary and a number of nearby harbours.

15
The last private owners – the Nairn family

THE HARBOUR THE NAIRNS FOUND

In November 1928, Sir Michael Nairn, Bart, bought Elie House Estate, which included the harbour, from Captain William James Baird. Captain Baird had inherited the estates which William Baird had bought in 1853. Sir Michael was the head of the famous linoleum-manufacturing family.

As he reviewed his new acquisition, one of Sir Michael's early thoughts, on finding out how little use was made of the harbour, was that the employment of a full-time harbour master was not justified. There was no longer any passenger traffic at all and very little cargo traffic. The harbour dues to be collected from the few pleasure craft and fishing boats using the harbour did not produce enough revenue even to pay the harbour master's wages, never mind the costs of maintenance work that might be needed.

A possible problem was that one of the harbour master's duties was to service the navigation light at the pierhead. Since 1868 it had been kept lit overnight through every winter from October to march. Sir Michael's agent wrote to the Northern Lighthouse Board to find out if there was any formal requirement for him to maintain this light. Their reply is not among the surviving estate papers, but Sir Michael decided that he would continue the light for one more year. The light was not lit after 1929, and the installation decayed until it was finally removed in World War II. A part-time harbour master continued to be employed until the harbour was handed over to the Town Council in 1955.

Sir Michael found that there were some arrears of maintenance work to undertake, particularly in the granary. In 1930 the roof had to be completely re-slated, and all the windows replaced, at a total cost of £350. The robust main structures of the pier, the quay and the causeway required little attention, except in respect of fittings like the iron ladders. On one of their earlier designs for reconstructing the pier the Stevensons had commented that a substantially wider pier would be much more capable of resisting the force of the heavy seas than the old narrow pier. The outer end of the old pier had broken down in 1808, which led to a progressive collapse ultimately extending to 70 feet of its 170-foot length. The pier designed by John Moffat and completed in 1860 had proved the Stevensons were right. Though the odd stone had had to be re-set from time to time it had required substantial repairs only once in 1884.

HARBOUR USE UNDER THE NAIRNS

In the first one or two years of Nairn ownership there were still occasional shipments of potatoes, but these soon stopped. Otherwise there were no great changes in the use of the harbour in the 27 years it was owned by the Nairns. Before World War II one or two sizeable yachts and a few smaller pleasure craft and boats belonging to local fishermen were the principal users. The charges were small and produced little revenue.

The harbour provided some accommodation used by the fishers who rented from the estate the rights to set fixed salmon nets off the estate's shores. These rights were usually let to firms from Johnshaven or Montrose. For a number of years a Johnshaven netsman rented part of the granary and the disused weigh-house (17) to store his gear, and also had the use of a net-drying ground (18) on the dune to the west of the causeway. One of the houses of the Toft was let as a salmon bothy which housed the netsmen during the fishing season.

WORLD WAR II

The limitations of Elie Harbour meant that it had no significant part to play in the many military activities going on in Fife and the Forth estuary during the Second World War, though there were several notable developments along the nearby shore.

The most striking military buildings in the area were the massive concrete emplacements for a 6-inch gun battery on Kincraig. This 2-gun battery, installed in 1939 together with a similar battery at

Archerfield on the opposite shore behind Fidra, commanded the entrance to the middle Firth at the first narrowing of the estuary, across a gap of about 8 miles. An emplacement was built for a third gun, which the official records indicate was installed in 1943. A gunner who served at the battery in 1946 told Ron Morris there were only two guns at that date. On the landward side of Kincraig the slope was terraced to create sites for the magazines and hutments to accommodate the gunners. Pill-boxes, machine-gun posts, and barbed-wire fences and entanglements were sited to protect the battery.

Large concrete anti-tank blocks were put in place round the shore a little above high-water mark at any places where tank landings might be attempted. A few of them have been left in place on Elie Ness in the north-east corner of Wood Haven. Near Boat Wynd, in the face of the low cliff of Chapel Ness where it meets the beach, a pill-box for a machine-gun post was constructed to command the beach in front of Earlsferry. The aperture for the gun is shown in the illustration (27). Close to the harbour, where the Loch Run debouches on to the shore, a concrete tank was constructed at the base of the sea wall to intercept the run and form a small reservoir for fire-fighting during air raids. On Elie Ness, the hydrophone huts of the First World War were brought back into service for their original purpose, but there was no boom defence across the estuary until west of Inchkeith.

On Admiralty orders the Thill Rock buoy was once again removed at the beginning of the war. After the war it was re-established as a large red can buoy, still unlit at this period.

The three ancient cannon, one of which is shown in the photograph (17) from much earlier in the century, and one field gun of Boer War vintage, which had been a feature of the Law for many years, were removed about this time in one of the drives to collect scrap-iron for the war effort. It was probably part of the same scrap-iron drive that took away the remains of the pierhead light. The photograph also shows the roof of the weigh-house, and fishing boats drawn up above high water at Lucky's Hole.

During the war the harbour was no doubt occasionally used by naval craft, but unlike the other active harbours in the vicinity it did not have the facilities to be very useful to the Royal Navy.

A Valentine postcard registered in August 1944, but perhaps from a photograph taken a little earlier, shows the wartime harbour (28). The pierhead light has not yet been removed for scrap; and the mooring of the boats shows the relatively haphazard pattern resulting from individual owners laying moorings in allocated spaces. This practice, later with a good many more boats, persisted until 1969, when the first chains establishing regular tiers of moorings were laid.

THE RISE OF RECREATIONAL SAILING
After the war, it was evident to the estate's owners that in the future the predominant use of the harbour would be for recreational sailing. In September 1948, pursuing this theme, the factor wrote to North Berwick Town Council to ask about their mooring charges and charges for visiting boats. The letter noted that the craft that visited Elie were principally 3-ton to 5-ton motor vessels. The great expansion of yachting and dinghy sailing in the Forth was still some time in the future. The harbour dues continued to produce very little revenue.

At this period, in sailing centres all around the Forth there was growing interest in dinghy sailing and racing. Some young and not-so-young Elie residents and regular visitors played a large part in this, and interest was stimulated by the introduction of new and cheaper classes of dinghy. A major stimulus came from the successes of competitors from Forth centres, including Elie, in Scottish, British and international competitions. More small yachts and motor-boats were also brought into the harbour by Elie residents, second-home-owners and visitors.

The expansion of small-boat sailing, and the estate's recognition that the granary would never be used again for its original purpose, led to an interesting modification of the north gable overlooking the harbour. A wide doorway was cut in the wall of the first floor, and a strong steel beam was inserted above it, projecting out far enough to allow blocks and tackle to be fitted to enable small boats to be hoisted up for storage over the winter on an upper floor.

In 1951, when Mr. Alex McLeod took up the post of factor to the extensive Nairn estates, he found that the now elderly Sir Michael, resident at Elie House, took a keen interest in all that went on at the harbour. Every Saturday morning, when conditions were suitable, the factor called at Elie

House, and took the place of the chauffeur to drive Sir Michael to the harbour for an inspection. One of the laird's main concerns was to see that the iron stanchion and chain barrier that fenced round the corner where the pier met the quay, to prevent pedestrians from falling in, was kept in good condition.

THE CLOSING OF THE SLUICES

Until 1951 the sluices constructed in 1912 had continued to function effectively in limiting the build -up of sand in the harbour. In that year, during a violent storm, powerful surges through one of the sluices drove a yacht berthed alongside from its moorings to ground on the harbour beach, causing it to become a virtual wreck in the process. Sir Michael decided that the sluices should be blocked to prevent a similar accident in the future. Heavy concrete walls were put in place to close the outer openings of the sluices. The effect over time was to accelerate the accumulation of sand in the harbour, particularly against the pier and in the corner by the granary. In 1953 part of the blocking wall was removed from the sluice nearest the granary, which made some improvement but still left a problem.

A PRESENT FOR THE TOWN COUNCIL

In 1952, following the death of Sir Michael, his son Sir George had succeeded to the estate. He did not wish to live in Elie House, which was sold. A year or so later, reviewing the affairs of the harbour, Sir George saw it as a liability, but recognised that it was providing a public service. Not only was it open to all vessels suitable to use it, and in that sense though it was privately-owned it was a public harbour, it was also a traditional and popular place of public resort.

The estate had continued to keep the harbour structures and the granary in repair. The costs of management and maintenance of the harbour exceeded the very small receipts from harbour dues and granary rents. Legal advice on the level of dues that could be charged referred back to the limits set by the schedule of dues in the 1857 Act; but these concerned the commercial use of the harbour and it appeared there were no restrictions on the dues that might be charged for the use of the harbour by yachts and other pleasure craft.

Against that background Sir George concluded that the harbour as a public service might be more appropriately owned and run by a public body, which might be able to develop its recreational use in a more active way than the estate felt able to do; and he instructed his factor to open discussions with the Town Council.

In August 1954, Mr. McLeod wrote to the Council to ask if they would be willing to accept the harbour, with the granary and the adjoining land, as a gift in memory of Sir George's father. Before this formal offer was made there had been exchanges between the parties, in the course of which the factor had drawn up a detailed statement of harbour revenue and expenditure over the period of five years from 1948 to 1952.

Excluding a number of one-off items, such as the modification of the north gable of the granary and closing and part re-opening the sluices, the factor estimated that the annual cost of maintenance of the harbour and the granary averaged about £18, rates about £12, and harbour master's wages £52, a total expenditure of £82 per year. Income in rents and harbour dues averaged about £45 a year. He put the estate's annual loss on the harbour, taking one year with another, at £30 or so. The Council seem to have taken the view that to keep the harbour running would inevitably entail one-off expenditures from time to time, for they added back the factor's excluded items to arrive at an estimated annual loss of £70 to £100. This figure did not deter the Council. The Minutes record that "In view of its value to the amenity of the burgh the Council agreed to accept the Conveyance of the Harbour".

The Council were required to obtain the approval of the Secretary of State for Scotland before they could accept the offer. Approval was duly given after it had been confirmed that none of the local authorities in the area had any objections to the transfer of ownership. The harbour had been owned by the lairds of Ardross and later of Elie since records began: it had now become public property.

16
Fishing in the 20th century

FISHING AT EARLSFERRY – THE LAST YEARS
Fishing had been important to Earlsferry from time immemorial; and its two small harbours were being used by fishermen until well into the 20th century. At least three fishing families had kept boats in the inlet beside the old ferry pier below Chapel Ness in the early years of the century, and one or two boats were still kept there after World War II. Despite its decrepit state, the old pier with its iron mooring rings and a single stone pawl (a bollard) still standing was quite useful for small rowing boats practising line-and-creel-fishing.

The early 20th century photograph (3) of Earlsferry House, now long demolished, shows a yawl moored at the ferry inlet. The pier appears as a dark line of partly tumbled stones behind the yawl, which is moored fore-and-aft as was necessary for boats lying in the narrow inlet. The obviously posed photograph (7) shows two smaller boats in the Cockstail Rocks harbour, which continued to be used by Earlsferry fishermen until the early 1950s. In the 30s and 40s there were usually about six boats there used for line-fishing, mainly for codling and flounders, and creel-fishing for crabs and lobsters using line-caught mackerel as bait. For the whitefish the bait was lugworm dug from the foreshore.

Writing in 1930, in his otherwise comprehensive account *Fishing Boats and Fisher Folk on the East Coast of Scotland*, Peter F. Anson passes straight from Largo to St. Monans as if there was no fishing at all at Earlsferry or Elie. He says only that Elie Bay - he does not use the word harbour - "*in rough weather affords a safe anchorage for fishing craft*". This is a curious gap in a book which includes details of many harbours much smaller than Elie. Anson's main interest is in the impressive craft that pursued the herring fishing, mainly not far offshore along the coast from Shetland to East Anglia, but could also go further afield in pursuit of whitefish. These larger craft were not represented in Elie or Earlsferry. There is evidence that Earlsferry fishermen took part in this large-scale fishing in the

18th century, in the record of the sad loss of seven men when a single Earlsferry boat went down; but there is no evidence of large boats being used in the 20th century.

The small boats that continued to use the two Earlsferry harbours could not carry large fleets of creels; but in the first half of the century lobsters and crabs were plentiful and a stock of 20 creels would produce worthwhile catches to take to market in Anstruther. The line-caught fish were sold in the neighbourhood from baskets carried from door-to-door by the fishermen or their wives or other family members.

At the Cockstail Rocks the boats were moored both in the creek between the two rock ledges that formed the harbour, and in the more open water on the Chapel Ness side of the western ledge. The aerial view (4) shows four small boats moored on the west side of the harbour, and one or perhaps more in the narrow inlet itself. These moorings offered little shelter in southerly winds, and when the weather was threatening the fishermen would combine to drag all the boats up above high-water mark. This was a major factor limiting the size of boats they could use.

In the first half of the century there were very few fishermen working from Elie Harbour, by then used mainly by pleasure boats. Earlsferry had always had the larger fishing community. In earlier times this was perhaps partly because the Earlsferry harbours belonged to the burgh, which did not charge residents any harbour dues, whereas at Elie, as at other privately-owned Scottish harbours, the proprietor was entitled one of every ten fish landed, known as "*teind fish*". In later years *teind* fish had been foregone, and the dues the estate charged to fishermen at Elie were very low, perhaps as little as 10/- a year for a small boat.

Among the factors helping to preserve small boat line-fishing until well into the 20th century were the restrictions placed on North Sea and distant-water fishing by the two World Wars. The effect was perhaps more marked in World War II, when enemy action had made the North Sea even more dangerous for fishing boats, than in World War I. The introduction of rationing from the outset of the war was also a factor: this led to a strong demand for locally-caught fish.

A FISHING LIFE

The great changes that effectively ended the old way of fishing in the area can be illustrated by an account of the working life of one of the fishermen descendants of an old Earlsferry fishing family. James Linton's mother was a Webster, and his uncle William Webster was the last Earlsferry fisherman to practise line-fishing from a rowing-boat based at the Cockstail Rocks (4, 7), and hawk his catch of codling and flounders from a basket to his old-established customers in the neighbourhood.

Jimmy Linton, now one of the oldest survivors of the fishing community of Earlsferry, acquired his first boat in 1940, at the age of fourteen. It was one of a pair of boats, each not much more than ten feet long, made by a fisherman friend of his family from a double-ended boat by the simple procedure of sawing it in two and fitting a transom to each of the cut ends. Jimmy was able to buy one half for 2/6. It still needed some work, but the finished product gave good service, and enabled him to begin fishing on his own account. This became a spare-time activity after he took up an apprenticeship, training to be a marine engineer at Smiths, Marine Engineers in Anstruther.

Line-fishing of the traditional kind did not seem likely to offer much of a future, and engineering seemed more promising; but from his first purchase in 1940 Jimmy was never to be without a boat and the means to go fishing. It was sometime, however, before he became a full-time fisherman.

Early in his apprenticeship he used his boat as much for the pleasure of enjoying a row as for fishing, and it was while taking a friend out on the water that he had a very alarming experience, which led him on 31 July, 1941, to a remarkable rescue. Rowing in the West Bay near the beacon he saw an aeroplane in flames come hurtling over Kincraig to crash into the sea nearby. It was a Blackburn Roc from HMS Jackdaw, the naval air station at Crail, which had been on a low-flying exercise in Largo Bay and had struck some of the many poles which had been planted in the bay between high and low

water as obstacles to invasion by air or sea. The plane had a crew of three.

Before the Roc dived into the water two crewmen, both wrapped in flames, had jumped, but the pilot was still in the plane. The crewmen were already dead by the time Jimmy had rowed to the scene; but he was able, reaching over the stern of his small boat, to extricate the barely conscious pilot from the plane, while his friend trimmed the boat by sitting in the bow. The pilot was too heavy to be got into the boat, but though barely conscious was just able to cling on to the stern while Jimmy rowed to the shore. Fortunately the sea was reasonably calm.

When they reached the beach at the point where the cart track across the golf course meets the shore, an ambulance was waiting. Gunners at the 6-inch battery on Kincraig had seen the incident, and been able to call the ambulance which took the injured pilot off to hospital.

It was a surprise to Jimmy to learn later that the pilot's father was Sir George Wilkinson, Bart., who was at the time the Lord Mayor of London, holding that office in the first year of the Blitz. Jimmy still has the wristwatch which the Lord Mayor came to Elie to present to him, engraved with a suitable inscription to commemorate his rescue.

David Wilkinson returned to active duty, and appears to have had an eventful career, in which his services earned him the Distinguished Service Cross. A distinction of which he was probably less proud was to take off in a hurry from an aircraft carrier with an engineer sitting on the fuselage in front of the tailfin clinging on desperately. With this impediment Wilkinson could not land back on the carrier, but was fortunate to be able to bring his plane and the engineer safely to land at a nearby airfield. He succeeded his father as the 2nd Baronet, and died in 1972.

Jimmy's apprenticeship was interrupted by military service, but after demobilisation he returned to Smiths to complete his time and qualify as a marine engineer. In 1950 he joined James Miller's boatyard in St. Monans. For the next ten years fishing could only be a part-time pursuit, but he was never without a boat.

In 1955 he joined the Coastguard Service as an Auxiliary Coastguard. He continued in the Service until 1986, latterly as the officer-in-charge of the

Elie Station, succeeding his brother Sandy in that post, which he had taken up about 1980, when the last full-time coastguards were withdrawn.

In 1960 Jimmy decided that fishing still offered good opportunities for someone who was willing to work at it; but the old style practised in his family for generations could no longer provide a living. Two main forms of fishing remained significant in the Elie area. These were creel-fishing, with much larger fleets of pots than in earlier years, and fishing with fixed nets extending from the shore at carefully chosen locations to trap migrating salmon, grilse, and sea-trout. Fishing of this type had been carried on along the Fife coast for centuries, by fishermen renting concessions from the estates that owned the fishing rights.

In the Elie area fishermen from Johnshaven and Montrose had rented the salmon rights for many years; but in 1960 the rights came up for renting anew, and Jimmy was able, for rents totalling only £5 a year, to acquire rights over several stretches of shore reaching from Kirkcaldy almost to St. Monans. However, it was only the area from Largo to Elie Ness that was still being worked, from four traditional stations, two in Largo Bay, one in the West Bay, and one at Apple Rock by the harbour.

The salmon fishermen also rented parts of the granary to store their gear. Renting the rights entitled the fishermen to dry their nets on frames erected on the nearby shore. At Elie Harbour the nets were dried on poles set up above high water on the harbour beach, as shown in the photograph (18).

The nets, referred to in statute as "*fixed engines*" were of three types, but all had the common feature of a "*leader*", a long high net stretching at right angles to the shore to block the passage of the migrating fish moving up the estuary in search of their spawning river. As the fish turned away from the shore to get round the obstacle they were guided by nets stretching from the outer end of the leader part-way to the shore to swim into enclosures from which they could not turn back, where they were collected by the fishermen. Over sand, the nets were fixed on poles: at a rock station they were stretched from rings on the rock to an anchor and a vertical spreading spar at the outer end.

The nets were of three kinds. Stake-nets were simply based on the sand, and the fish were lifted out by large landing nets on long staffs: fly-nets had net bottoms at the trap ends, which could be hauled up to enable the fish to be removed. At rock stations it was of course necessary to use nets with net bottoms, of a pattern known as bag-nets. Jimmy used fly-nets on his three sand stations, and a bag-net at the Apple Rock. He knew from the remains of net poles in the sand of Elie town beach that in earlier times there had been nets there; but this station had long been abandoned. The season for fishing with fixed nets in this way extended from January to August. For part of the rest of the year Jimmy fished with creels for lobsters and crabs.

For a number of years the salmon fishing was successful, as stocks of fish were good. In his best year, 1976, he caught about 2,500 salmon, as well as hundreds of sea-trout and grilse; but from that year catches declined: the explanations of the great fall in salmon stocks in Scottish rivers are complex. In 1986 Jimmy caught only 60 salmon.

At this point he abandoned salmon-fishing, and turned his attention entirely to creel-fishing for lobsters and crabs, by then the main form of commercial fishing from the harbour. The photograph (29) shows his fine lobster-boat, the Provider II, KY153, the product of a conversion job of which he is justly proud. Jimmy finally retired from fishing in 2002, at the age of seventy-six. One or two boats still use Elie Harbour for creel-fishing. Part of a fleet of creels on the pier is shown in the illustration (30), alongside the modern yachts which have become the predominant users of the harbour.

After long centuries in which line-fishing from small boats had supported many families in Elie and Earlsferry, by the 1980s there was no more fishing of this type, except in season for mackerel, almost exclusively for creel bait. A way of life that had long endured had finally come to an end.

30. The dual-purpose harbour c.1995

31. The donkey-man - 1950s

17
Under Town Council management

THE TOWN COUNCIL'S SEASHORE

RESPONSIBILITIES

Before the Town Council became the owners of the harbour they had had important responsibilities concerning the shore. While the foreshore adjoining the town of Elie was owned by Elie estate, the foreshore of Earlsferry, including the two old harbours, had been owned by the Town Council of Earlsferry. Its ownership passed in 1929 to the new joint Council, formed that year by the amalgamation of the Councils of the two burghs. Above high-water mark (defined in old titles as "*the full sea*", later interpreted as Mean High Water Mark Ordinary Spring Tides MHWOST) the beach adjoining the town gardens was usually owned by the adjoining proprietor.

By the 1920s the annual letting of the right to gather seaware and payments per ton of sand removed from the beach had become the only sources of revenue from the shore for Earlsferry. No harbour dues were collected. At Elie, only the proprietor of the estate could make charges for seaware or sand, and he received the harbour dues.

One of the early acts of the new joint Town Council was to make Sea Beach Bye-laws, effective from 17 September 1931. These aimed to protect the environment; to prohibit personal behaviour that might cause annoyance; to regulate shooting, fishing, and the playing of games; and to control commercial activities. Their general tone is reflected in the new bye-laws of 1954 which replaced those of 1931. 12 of the main 15 articles contain the potent words "*no person ....shall ....,*" sometimes qualified by the phrase "*without the special permission of the magistrates*". For many years "*the special permission of the magistrates*" was given to Mr. Robert Haig to "ply ponies for hire upon the beach". Mr. Haig's ponies and donkeys were a much loved feature of holidays in Elie and Earlsferry for many generations of children. It was a condition annually set out in the Town Council minutes that "*no complaints were received about*

animal droppings on the beach." The photograph (31) shows Mr. Haig with his stable of ten donkeys and ponies, some customers - one of whom does not seem entirely happy - and his usual team of teenage helpers whose services were rewarded by the fun of looking after the animals and the occasional free ride.

The joint Council continued to raise revenue from the collection of seaware, let by the year; and permits for the removal of sand were issued, charged at 1/6 per ton. After the council became the owners of Elie Harbour seaware and sand from the harbour area were offered on the same basis as at Earlsferry.

The Council also gave permission for a boat hirer to offer trips round the bay. He operated from a temporary floating wooden gangway near the breakwater ramp at the west end of South Street as shown in the illustration (32).

In April 1954 the Council, in exercise of its responsibility for the roads in the burgh, had to carry out a costly piece of work to protect the retaining seawall supporting the road along the front of the Toft. To prevent the wall being undercut, the Council had its base re-inforced with concrete, forming a projecting toe to resist the action of the waves. One of the first actions of the Council's new harbour Committee, which was established before the formal transfer of ownership of the harbour was complete, was to move the Council to prohibit the removal of sand from this area

THE TOWN COUNCIL TAKE OVER

The Town Council became the owners of the harbour in April 1955, and erected a plaque on the wall of the pier with the following inscription:

THIS HARBOUR WAS GIFTED
TO THE TOWN COUNCIL
OF THIS BURGH
BY
SIR MICHAEL GEORGE NAIRN BART.
IN MEMORY OF HIS FATHER
SIR MICHAEL NAIRN BART.
OF ELIE HOUSE ESTATE
1955

The Council owned and operated the harbour until 1975. Under their ownership the harbour continued to be kept in good repair; but throughout the period the granary was a source of some concern, as its condition deteriorated and the cost of maintenance and occasional modifications exceeded the rents received. The Council employed a part-time Pier Attendant (sometimes referred to as the Harbour Master) through the summer months to collect car parking fees and harbour dues and supervise moorings.

Pleasure craft, including yachts, dinghies, catamarans and small motor-boats continued to be the main users. The only commercial use of the harbour was by a few boats fishing almost exclusively for crabs and lobsters. Boats engaged in fishing were usually given preference for berths in the deepest part of the harbour beside the pier, where they could load and unload their creels and their catches. There were usually some keep-boxes moored in the bay below low-water mark, where catches could be kept until enough crabs and lobsters had been collected to take to market.

CONDITION OF THE PIER AND THE GRANARY

The Council's first act was to commission a report on the pier from the Aberdeen Civil Engineers, Archibald Henderson and Partners, who reported that it was in good condition. They mentioned one or two minor problems, such as cavities in the wall near the pier head, and some disturbed setts, all of which they considered could be repaired for about £25. They also said that if it were ever decided to grout the gaps between the setts in the deck of the pier it would be essential to leave vents to relieve any water pressure underneath generated by wave action forcing water through the outer wall of the pier. The minor repairs were carried out. No action was taken to grout up the setts. Parking on the pier was forbidden.

This advice from the engineers relates to a key question about the structure of the pier. Was it built as a wash-through pier, with openings left between the stones to allow water to enter and pass freely through, or were the stones bound together with mortar to form an impermeable barrier? For many years there was no pointing between the large stone blocks facing the pier on all sides, which provided many openings allowing water to enter. When it has been necessary to open excavations in the pier it has been apparent that the hearting has not been consolidated into a form of concrete but at least for the most part is merely compacted together. This led to the view that the structure is designed to be a wash-through pier, certainly as far as the main structure built in the 19th century goes. Whether the buried stones of what remains of the 1600 structure inside the modern pier (2) are bonded together by mortar is not so apparent. The 1600 pier was not very wide, and it seems unlikely it would have been strong enough to have stood as long as it did if it had not been consolidated with mortar bonding the stones. The fact that the exposed outer end of the pier resisted over two hundred years of battering and erosion by the sea and the weather before it collapsed does not suggest that it had been held in place all those years by gravity alone.

In April 1956 the iron ladders at the pier were noted to be in good condition; and the last elements of the structure which reflected its long use as a cargo handling pier were taken away when the Council decided that the long vertical timber fenders (25) that had protected the cargo ships lying alongside should be removed. From then on, the fishing boats and other craft lying at the pier would provide their own fenders, which almost invariably took the form of old tyres.

The granary was inspected by the Harbour Committee, who reported that it was generally in sound condition, but that the stairs and landing were in need of repair. Despite that finding, just two years later, in April 1957 after there had been some heavy winter gales, it was observed that the north gable was leaning outward at the top and repairs were instructed. When the granary was built, around 1805, as was then standard practice in buildings of its form, a long iron tie-rod had been inserted a little below the apex of the gable through the length of the building to secure iron plates on the outer faces of the gables to prevent just such a movement; but it appears that weather erosion of the mortar between the stones had weakened their adhesion sufficiently to allow some movement of the stones above the anchor-point. The outward list of the top of the gable remained throughout the Council's ownership, but without any further movement being detected.

Harbour Committee – Revenue and Charges

Even before it had taken over the harbour the Town Council had appointed a harbour committee, which was to be responsible for the management of the harbour under the Council's supervision and subject to approval on material issues and questions of expenditure and charges. At its first meeting, in February 1955 the Committee began a review of charges, ruled that the storage in the granary should be restricted to boats and their gear, and instructed that the salmon-fishers who used parts of the granary to store and repair their gear should be restricted to a defined area, instead of spreading their activities all over the place.

The Harbour Master was re-appointed at 17/6 per week (compared with £1 per week under Nairn ownership.) The question of finding and retaining a Harbour Master at a weekly rate the harbour revenues could support was frequently a problem for the Council throughout its ownership of the harbour. (In 1974, when the Council were about to hand over the harbour to a newly-formed local company, his pay had risen to £10 per week plus 20% of the dues collected.) An area was defined for the parking of buses at 3/- per bus per day.

Perhaps with the object of boosting harbour revenues, the Council decided that day-long parking of buses on the High Street beside the churchyard should no longer be permitted. The charge for buses at the harbour was raised to 5/- per day before the end of the year. The Council also ruled that no cars were to be parked on any part of the seashore. (This rule could not preclude those owners of houses whose titles included land down to the high water mark from parking cars or allowing others to park on the land by the shore that they owned.) The Council later agreed that buses and cars might park on the harbour road as well as at the harbour itself. Car parking charges were subsequently set at 6 pence per day, and an annual charge was fixed for visitor's boats at £3 per annum. No mention is made in the records of charges for residents' boats.

As a result of the Committee's further reviews the Council later issued a new schedule of harbour dues, completely different from the last formal schedule published by the estate in 1884. That schedule had followed the pattern first set by the Royal Charter of 1601, with heavy emphasis on import and export cargoes, the landing of fish, and the coming and going of cargo ships and fishing boats. The Council's schedule, a later version of which is reproduced here (33), dealt exclusively with the mooring, launching, and storage of boats, including the storage of boats and their gear in the granary.. It will be noted it applied only to visitors' boats.

Paying for moorings entitled the boat-owner to free car-parking; but others had to pay. Over the years the Council had difficulty with the question whether ratepayers should be required to pay for moorings. In 1958 they were required to pay 5/- per annum: in June 1966 the Council minutes record that "*it was confirmed*" Elie ratepayers were exempted from paying dues at the harbour.

One source of income had come to an end by 1958. Farmers no longer wished to collect seaware to manure their fields or certainly not to pay for collecting it and the Council had to pay to have it removed from the harbour.

Boundaries and Road Responsibilities

Early in their ownership of the harbour the Council set in train negotiations to buy a small parcel of land adjoining the causeway. This was a part of the large grassy dune on the west side of the causeway that had not existed before the causeway was built and had accumulated steadily over the decades until it became an extensive area covered in marram and other grasses and plants. The land conveyed to the Town Council by the Nairn family had been defined by a straight boundary line from the end of the pier to the eastern end of the land of the Coastguard Station, and a substantial part of the dune lay to the west of the line. It had never been part of the estate owned by the Nairns, but had remained Baird property.

In April 1957 the Council were disappointed to be told that the ground had been sold to Mr. Ovenstone of Braehead Cottage just across the road, a property which had been in the Ovenstone family since the 18th century. The Ovenstones had a long association with the harbour as ship-owners, shipmasters, merchants, pilots and seamen. John Ovenstone, an Elie skipper, had been one of the party which Sir John Anstruther had mistakenly sent off in one of his boats to take welcoming gifts to John Paul Jones in 1779, when he was raiding shipping round the coast of Britain in the American War of Independence. Six Ovenstones with seafaring occupations had signed the petition to the laird in the 1830s about the condition of the harbour.

In 1958 the Town Council took issue with the County Council, which had resolved to delete the road from the Toft to the pier from their list of highways. In January 1959 the two Councils agreed that the County Council would put the road into repair until the burgh boundary was extended to take in the harbour. Once that was done the road would become the burgh's responsibility, like the other roads in Elie.

Up until December 1959 the harbour had been outside the burgh boundary which had ended on the east at the west boundary of the harbour land, described above. As part of a larger boundary extension, formally approved by the Sheriff of Fife and Kinross on 18 December, the harbour and the nearby shore of Wood Haven and some of the adjoining land were included within the burgh.

MEASURES TO ATTRACT VISITORS

The Harbour Committee came to the view that more needed to be done to attract visitors and residents to the harbour, by providing facilities for games. In the spring of 1956 they put forward a set of proposals. These were to create a putting course on the rough land between the quay, the Law, and the eastern wall of the causeway; to lay some concrete draught boards; to form a skittle alley in the granary; and to purchase 6 rowing boats for hire. The Council approved the putting green and the rowing boats but drew the line at the other two proposals. In the event only the putting green went ahead.

There appeared to be some overlap of jurisdiction between the Council's long-established Beach Committee and the Harbour Committee. It was the Beach Committee that decided that bathing boxes should be permitted at the harbour beach, in the same style as at the main town beach, and also that sand should be sold from the harbour all summer.

The putting green was opened in the summer of 1957, and the charge was fixed by the Harbour Committee at 3 pence per round. That year revenue was raised by letting the right to sell refreshments at the harbour in the summer for £15. It appears

that things were looking up on the revenue front, which emboldened the Council to appoint a "*pier attendant*" for the summer at £4 per week plus 20% of all revenues produced from the pier, the harbour, the harbour land, and the granary.

The Town Council decided at the end of 1958 to convert the putting course into a car park, and, the equipment was sold to St. Monans Town Council. Liaison arrangements between the two Councils were not difficult to make. They shared the same Town Clerk.

In 1956 the Council began to discuss the possibility of allowing travelling showmen to set up a roundabout and other shows at the harbour for the summer season. The issue was considered too sensitive for quick discussion and deferred for consultation and the consideration of objections.

In 1958 the Council received £9 for the right to sell refreshments at the harbour, using the weigh-house as a kiosk; and in 1959 the concession was let to the Edinburgh branch of Walls for £18 for the season. Walls continued to operate the concession until 1962, when it was again advertised. The old weigh-house continued in use as a refreshment kiosk for the rest of the Council's ownership of the harbour.

A further attempt to run a summer boat-hiring business was made in 1963, when a licence to be renewed on an annual basis was granted to the owner of the Ship Inn and a partner to run pleasure trips in motor-boats to carry up to 12 persons, subject to appropriate checks and compliance with all relevant safety regulations. It does not appear that this project was successful, as there is no reference in the Council minutes for any later year to the renewal of this licence.

The harbour beach was never used for pony and donkey rides. The last reference to those in the Council minutes comes in July 1972, when permission was granted to Mr. John Haig, the son of the earlier donkeyman (31), to work ponies for hire on the town beach, subject to the usual conditions, for a period of five years.

MOORINGS

During the Council's ownership moorings were managed by the Harbour Master, under the direction of the Harbour Committee whose Convener was available to deal with exceptional problems. Boats berthed alongside the pier posed no special problems, though there were sometimes disputes about the allocation of berths which the Harbour Committee had to resolve. Boats moored in the open water in the centre of the harbour, were attached to moorings laid by the boat-owners as directed.

The first step to providing fixed moorings was taken in March 1963 when a chain was laid, fixed to anchors donated by Captain Keir, parallel to the south wall of the harbour at a distance which allowed a single tier of boats to be moored there to running moorings. This was useful for the mooring of small boats and tenders.

In 1965 it appeared that the limit on the length of boats allowed to moor in the harbour had been 36 feet. The Convenor of the Harbour Committee reported to the Council in February of that year that he had, exceptionally, allowed two boats of 40 feet length to moor in the harbour. After 1969 the limit on length was reduced to 30 feet, to permit a new mooring plan that would make the maximum use of the space available. This plan required the laying of three heavy chains 165 feet long on lines parallel to the pier, attached at each end to concrete blocks. These chains allowed two tiers of yachts and motor-boats to be moored fore-and-aft, spaced so as to allow free passage between the tiers, between the front tier and the boats berthed at the pier, and between the inner ends of the tiers and the boats moored to the running moorings by the south wall. This development, later extended to three tiers (30) as one of the Council's last harbour improvements, fixed the general mooring plan of the harbour for the foreseeable future.

PUBLIC CONVENIENCES

A much-needed improvement in facilities for the public was initiated in 1967. Following instructions, the Burgh Surveyor submitted plans for a public convenience at the harbour, which he said was designed to be built "to withstand hard usage with minimum maintenance". He estimated the cost at £1,600, with the addition of £60 if electric light was provided. The proposal was approved and tenders for the work (including electric light) totalled £1,634 6 - 11. At a final cost of £1,670 - 7 - 7, this work was completed in 1968.

18
New life at the harbour

SAILING CLUB

In February 1964 the Town Council began discussions with a number of people, not all of them Elie residents, about the possible formation of a Sailing Club based at the harbour. The Council could see that the principal use of the harbour, for the foreseeable future, would be for recreational sailing and other water sports; and Elie harbour was well placed to attract sailors and would-be sailors from a wide area of Fife, if facilities were available. With this encouragement a group of enthusiasts set up the Elie and Earlsferry Sailing Club, whose members have constituted the most numerous group of harbour users ever since.

The Council made quite clear that they would remain the owners and would control the harbour, but they were ready to reach agreement with the Club on the facilities they would need. Early in its career the Club was able rent a small cottage adjoining the Ship Inn. The owner was willing to allow the Club to convert the interior of the building to suit its purposes, by providing changing accommodation and showers. The cottage later became the property of the Ship Inn, whose owners continued to be benevolent landlords.

Co-operation between the Club and the Council produced valuable results for both parties, for the Council by increasing the revenue from harbour usage, and for the Council as well as the Club by the development of minor elements of harbour infrastructure which facilitated the Club's activities. Liaison was helped by the Council's acceptance of an invitation from the Club for its harbour convener to become an *ex-officio* member of the Sailing Club Committee.

Over the years the Club ran many races, some being special named events with their own trophies, often combined into series, usually separate for dinghies and keel-boats. The Club kept the Town Council informed, particularly about the national and other open events which they were able to host from time to time.

In 1964 the Council leased to the Club one of the ground floor compartments of the granary for storage purposes. A year or so later the Club were able to tell the Council that they expected to host the Scottish Area GP14 Dinghy Racing Championship, and that they were putting emphasis on dinghy racing, partly as a means to encourage young people to take up sailing. This led in June 1968 to the Council giving permission to the Club to mark off an area of the dune near the newly-built public conveniences as a dinghy park. This permission did not become a formal lease until 1971, when the Club was authorised to fence the area; and in 1973 the Club was authorised to make the leased land into a concrete-surfaced hard-standing.

Later the Council gave permission to the Club to form a concrete launching slip at Lucky's Hole, the inlet in the rocks on the west side of Wood Haven at the landward end of the Law and the start of the causeway. This inlet had been traditionally used as a place to haul out fishing boats for the winter (17), but this had been long discontinued. A launching slip at this site would provide opportunities to launch boats into sheltered water under conditions where westerly winds made launching from the harbour beach impossible. For a variety of reasons the Club had not taken action on this permission before the Town Council ceased to exist; but the scheme was later carried out by the Town Council's successors in title, the Elie Harbour Company.

The success of the Scottish Area GP Championship event in 1969 led the Club into discussions about a much bigger event, which was the British OK Dinghy Championship of 1976. In 1971 the Club had informed the Council that they were being asked to stage this event. The Council were pleased to see their harbour being put on the national map in this way. This large meeting for single-handed dinghies was a great success, taking place the year after the Town Council had ceased to exist.

In July 1972, with the Council's co-operation, which extended to giving a reception for the participants, the Club was the host for the Scottish

32. Trips round the bay

ELIE HARBOUR CHARGES

PAYABLE IN ADVANCE

VISITORS' BOATS

YACHTS AND CABIN CRUISERS

UP TO 20 ft.

3/- per Day, 4/- per Night, 25/- per Week, 30/- per Fortnight, £2 10/- per month.

FROM 20 ft. to 36 ft.

4/- per Day, 6/- per Night, £1 10/- per week, £2 per Fortnight, £3 10/- per Month.

NO BOATS OVER 36 ft. to be allowed in Harbour.

RESIDENTS' BOATS

SAILING BOATS and MOTOR BOATS up to 16 ft.

5/- per Week, £2 10/- per Annum.

YACHTS and CABIN CRUISERS from 16 ft. to 30 ft.

6/- per week, £4 per Annum.

ROWING BOATS up to 12 ft.

4/- per week, £1 10/- per Annum.

100% is surcharged on all Boats belonging to Non-Residents and on all Boats used for Commercial Purposes.

ALL THE ABOVE CHARGES INCLUDE PARKING FEES.

STORAGE IN GRANARY

Boats over 14 ft. £1 15/-   Other Boats £1 5/-.   Boat's Gear £1 all per Annum.

"KEY FOR DEPOSITING GEAR DURING SEASON."   15/- will be charged and 15/- refund on return of key will be made.

BOATS LAUNCHED FROM BEACH

SAILING DINGHIES, MOTOR BOATS, SPEED BOATS, ROWING BOATS, CANOES, PUNTS, 3/- per day.

STORAGE OF BOATS ON HARBOUR, BEACH OR GRASS

Boats up to 16 ft. 10/-.   Boats over 16 ft. 1/- per foot extra.

NOTICE OF CONDITIONS :—BOATS and their Contents and Gear are admitted to ELIE HARBOUR, PIER and GRANARY, AT OWNERS' RISK ONLY, and the Town Council accept no responsibility for moorings.

NO BOATS ALLOWED TO MOOR AT STEPS WHICH MUST BE KEPT CLEAR OF MOORING ROPES.

D. C. COOK, *Town Clerk*, ELIE.

33. Harbour charges - 1960

National Power Boat Race Meeting. This went very well; and it left the Club with a handsome set of tall orange racing buoys, which subsequently adorned the bay for the Club's own races for a number of years.

A minor issue sparked by a clash of interests between harbour users rose in 1970 when a sea-angler who fished from the end of the pier complained that sailing boats leaving the harbour were sailing through and catching up his lines. At the same time some boat owners complained that they had been put at some risk by flying fishing tackle, with metal lures, weights and hooks being hurled out from the pierhead while they were sailing past. On enquiring, the Council were satisfied that long-distance casting (said to be up to 200 feet) was obstructing the legitimate use of the harbour. They forbade rod-fishing from the pier. In practice small boys with 6-foot rods and some older anglers with similar tackle were not disturbed.

Sand Clearance

An important improvement to the harbour in which the Sailing Club played a leading role, in co-operation with the Council, was the re-opening of the harbour sluices. By the late 1960s, following the closure of the sluices in 1953, the accumulation of sand in the harbour and against the pier had become a serious problem. This was of particular concern to the lobster fishermen, whose operations were restricted by the shorter and shorter periods for which there was enough water for their boats. The build-up of sand extended right across the harbour, and Sailing Club members were also much concerned. The Club pressed for action to be taken

The Club's Commodore, who was the Black Watch Major in charge of recruiting for the Army in Dundee, suggested that special military explosives, in the form of shaped charges, could be used to blast the blocking walls (one had already been partially removed) out into the sea. The Town Council did not favour this idea, fearing possible damage to the pier, and blast effects directed through the sluice tunnels towards the buildings of the Toft; but the possibility of taking advantage of military assistance in some other way was explored.

In 1974 the Town Council did authorise the Sailing Club to re-open both sluices fully. Club volunteers, greatly assisted in the heavy work by one robust fisherman, began the operation working at weekends when the tide permitted, but progress was slow. The work was eventually completed by a contractor employed by the Elie Harbour Company.

The effects of completely clearing the two sluices were quickly seen. Before the clearance the sand beside the pier was above the lowest rungs of the pier ladders. Soon afterwards it was observed that the level of the sand at the pier had fallen considerably; and since then it has generally remained below the level of the base of the sluice openings. The effect in keeping down the sand level extends to a considerable distance from the pier, but diminishes with increasing distance.

The granary

From an early date in the Council's ownership various proposals were brought forward to make better use of the granary, a large and solidly-built structure in which only a limited amount of space was put to use, for storage of boats and their gear, salmon nets, lobster creels, and other fishing gear. Use for some recreational purpose was mooted several times. In 1961 the Council decided to defer discussion of a proposal to turn it into a first-class hotel, and this idea seems to have been quietly dropped.

In 1964 the Sailing Club offered to lease part of the ground floor, and perhaps more, of the granary, and to put the leased part and the staircase into repair. The lease of part of the ground floor was agreed. The Club used this area for the storage of gear.

In March 1969 the Town Council received a letter from the Commodore on behalf of the Sailing Club offering to buy both the harbour and the granary for development for Sailing Club purposes. The Council minutes record that at the meeting at which this offer was considered the Provost took the unusual step of asking the Councillors round the table one by one to record their views. One after the other, they all said the offer should be rejected. In April 1969 the offer was repeated in a different form, as a proposal for a lease. The Councillors were unanimous in returning the same answer. These proposals did considerable damage to the hitherto amicable relations between the Council and the Club.

In 1970, after substantial repairs had been required to the granary roof, the Council obtained estimates for the development of the granary for recreation and tourism. An outline scheme costing perhaps about £12,000 was considered, for which it was learned it might be possible to obtain a Government grant of 75%, leaving £3,000 to be found locally. At this period the rents being received from the tenants of various parts of the granary totalled about £50 per year. There were frequent meetings with the Sailing Club, and other interested parties; but it became clear no support would be forthcoming from outside the Council for any ambitious project. In 1972 the work required simply to put the granary into proper repair was estimated to cost £6,200. Inquiry of the Scottish Development Department about the possibility of financial assistance elicited the reply that the granary was not of sufficient historical importance to warrant any grant from the Historic Building Council.

By late 1972, in the light of the Wheatley report on Local Government Reform, which recommended the abolition of all small burghs, the Town Council had agreed to consider any practicable steps to retain the harbour (including the granary) under the control of a local body. Not for the first time, *force majeure* was about to bring about a change in the ownership of the harbour.

THE COUNCIL'S LAST IMPROVEMENTS

Early in 1974 the Council authorised the burgh surveyor to install a davit near the end of the pier, for the use of the fishermen in hoisting nets, other gear, and their catches on to the pier. A davit was fabricated to the Burgh Surveyor's specification. It did work for a time; but a fisherman hoisting a heavy net found that, instead of the net coming up, the davit went down, and it had to be removed.

By early 1975 the Council's time was running out, but there was one last improvement that they wished to make before handing over the harbour. At their March meeting they authorised the installation of five street lights, at a cost not to exceed £2,000, the work to be completed by 9 May. As part of the same operation four floodlights were fixed to the walls of the granary to light the surrounding area, partly for security purposes. One of the Council's very last acts before demitting office for good was to approve a new schedule of harbour charges.

PLANNING FOR THE FUTURE

From 1972 onwards the Town Council gave increasing attention to the future of the granary, and later to that of the harbour itself. Under the Council's management the harbour had been kept in good repair; but throughout their ownership the granary was more a source of concern than a valuable asset, as its condition continued to deteriorate. The cost of maintenance, and some modifications to enable greater use to be made of it, considerably exceeded the rents received. The expedients the Council tried did not solve the problem.

The Council gave serious consideration to a proposal by a developer, who had already converted the granary at North Berwick harbour into flats, to buy the granary for the same purpose. If this scheme were to go ahead, alternative accommodation would be needed for existing granary users, including sheds for storing fishermen's gear, and possibly also covered storage for boats. The fishermen represented that they had a traditional right to dry nets on harbour land, and said they would wish to erect sheds on the site earlier used for that purpose. In the event the granary was not sold.

By March 1973 new proposals for the future of the harbour and the granary, prompted by the imminent re-organisation of local government, had begun to make progress in the Council. The key proposal was that in view of the forthcoming demise of the Council, a local Harbour Trust should be formed to take over the harbour, so that it would remain under local control.

At one stage, to ensure that the historic character of the harbour was preserved, the Council asked the National Trust for Scotland if the Trust would act as one of the harbour trustees; in the event an alternative way of achieving the same objective was found. The Council entered into a Conservation Agreement with the National Trust. This provided that no building or other structures should be erected on the harbour lands except such as were required in connection with the use of the harbour for fishing, sailing, and other recreational purposes; and the Trust's approval would be required for the plans and designs of any such buildings or structures. Similarly, structural alterations to the harbour and granary, both being listed as buildings of special architectural and historical interest, would not be undertaken without the approval of the Trust.

LOCAL CONTROL PRESERVED

In April 1974 the Council decided to transfer the harbour, the harbour lands, and the granary, with the exception of a small area including the public conveniences erected in 1968, to a new Trust. The Council would organise the setting-up of the Trust on the lines of the now well-established Isaac S. Mackie Trust, which had been established to provide sheltered housing in the town, and had shown how effective such a local body could be. The price to be paid to the Council for the property would be determined by the District Valuer. The Clerk to the Council was instructed to make preparations to set up the Trust.

By September 1974 matters were well advanced. The Council sought to identify possible sources of financial assistance to help the proposed Trust to carry out improvement works at the harbour. Replies received from the Scottish Sports Council and the Scottish Tourist Board suggested that some grants might be forthcoming if the Trust's constitution and its proposals met with their grant criteria.

Having explored the matter fully, the Council finally agreed in December 1974 to take the necessary action to have the Trust set up, also recording its intention that the cost of the property transaction would be met by a grant from the Council under the Physical Education and Training Act of 1937. To comply within the time available with all the legal requirements for the transfer, including those arising from the re-organisation of local government then underway, it was necessary to proceed in a slightly complicated way.

In the light of advice from the Inland Revenue, the proposed new body had to be constituted not as a trust but as a not-for-profit company limited by guarantee. The new body was called the Elie Harbour Company Limited, but in all essential respects its constitution and objects were the same as those proposed for the Trust. Three sitting councillors became directors of the new company (unpaid of course), and all the other councillors were invited to become members of the company, together with a number of other residents widely representative of the community, and harbour users and representatives of the fishermen and the Sailing Club. Additional directors were elected from among the members of the company.

The Town Council granted the newly-formed company a lease of the harbour, granary, and the harbour lands, always excepting the area including the public conveniences. The lease placed the company under the burdens and conditions in the Conservation Agreement; and it made clear that the Company were to carry on the management of the harbour for the same purposes as the Council had, in the same spirit and for the benefit of the community; and it included an option for the Company to buy the harbour at valuation. Generally, it gave the Company all the powers they needed to run the harbour.

The minutes of the Town Council's last meeting on 15 May 1975 record the grants that the Council had made to two local sports clubs and to Elie Harbour Company. The grants to the Company made use of the Council's powers under the Physical Training and Recreation Act 1937, the Civic Amenities Act 1967, and the Local Authorities (Historic Buildings) Act, 1962.

In view of a certain amount of controversy that had arisen over the scheme to retain local control over the harbour in the way they had chosen, the Council had taken the precaution of obtaining the opinion of senior Counsel on whether their proceedings in making the grants had been *intra vires*. Mr. Nicholas Fairbairn, Q.C., gave his opinion that not only were the Council's proceedings *intra vires*, but also that they had had a duty to act as they did if they considered their actions were in the best interests of the community of the burgh.

The grants were intended to promote the development of the harbour as a base for water sports of all kinds, for fishing, and for public recreation generally, and to assist in the preservation of the listed structures of the harbour and the granary. In total, the grants to the Company came to £12,000, which would not only enable the Company to buy the properties but give it valuable help in the discharge of its large responsibilities for substantial works of traditional construction in need of steady maintenance and with considerable potential for development.

On 7 May 1975 the Town Council sold the granary to the Company at the valuation of £1,000. Under the statutory provisions for local government re-organisation harbour powers were transferred to the new Regional Councils and Fife Regional

Council became the owners of Elie harbour, with the Company as their tenants.

When the Company approached the Regional Council asking to exercise its option under the lease to buy the harbour, the Regional Council initially wished to prevent or at least to postpone the sale; but the lease had been tightly drawn; and after a period of sometimes difficult discussions, and some controversy reported in the local press, the Company finally concluded the purchase of the harbour from the Council on 29 May 1979, at the District Valuer's price of £5,000.

The completion of the sale formalised the situation that had obtained in effect since May 1975. Within the important constraints imposed by the Conservation Agreement with the National Trust, and its status as a not-for-profit company, the Harbour Company had full powers to preserve, manage, and develop the harbour for its established users and for the benefit of the community. Local control had been preserved, with the directors and company members drawn from local residents and local harbour users. The Town Council had ensured that the Company started on its course with useful financial reserves, albeit small in relation to its large responsibilities, and with experienced former members of the Council on the Board to help set the Company on its way.

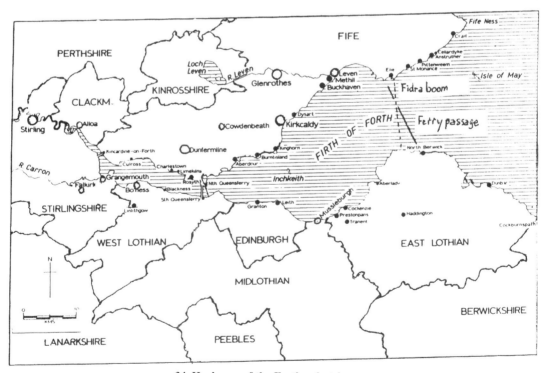

34. Harbours of the Forth - sketch map

An Overview

Through most of its existence Elie Harbour was the responsibility of successive owners of the lands of Ardross and Elie. Its fortunes had been greatly affected by the rise and sometimes the fall of the fortunes of five successive families. They included families descended from medieval aristocrats, from a lawyer and landowner who had been a key legal official for James VI, and from two families whose fortunes had come from industrial innovation and drive in the 19th century.

The last of the Dishington lairds, descended from a sister of Robert the Bruce, continued his father's work in the founding of the harbour in the 1590s, but then had to sell most of his lands to his wealthy lawyer father-in-law, William Scott, who completed the work. Before 1700, the Scotts had lost their estates partly because they had encumbered them with debt to raise money to support the failing Stuart dynasty.

At the end of Scotts' tenure, the harbour was in such poor condition that a collection for its repair was authorised in all the parish churches in Scotland. The enterprising Anstruther lairds who bought out the heavily indebted Scotts kept the harbour in reasonable repair until 1808, when it began to deteriorate.

For a number of years the harbour supported a shipyard, possibly from the 17th century or even earlier, which was still in operation in 1832. It was the base for local ship-owners, numbers of whom traded overseas. This trade appears to have been at its height around 1800, when there were seven large Elie owned ships in this trade, and considerable numbers of local men were employed at sea.

Under the last Anstruther laird, described by a contemporary as "a spend-thrift easy-dealing laird", the harbour fell into such a poor state that the Admiralty appointed a Commissioner to report on its condition; but nothing came of his damning report.

The restoration of the harbour to a fully-functioning condition by major works completed in 1860 was made possible by the sale of the indebted Anstruther estates in 1853 to a very rich industrial entrepreneur from the West of Scotland. William Baird, a leader in the ground-breaking industrial development of Scotland from the 1820s on, was responsible for the massive masonry structures that form the harbour in use today.

After 1860, very little changed at the harbour, except for the building, in 1889, of a timber paddle-steamer pier outside the stone pier. In 1928 the harbour was sold as part of Elie Estate by the Baird family to Sir Michael Nairn; and the Nairns continued to keep the harbour in good repair until 1955, when they presented it to the Town Council. Handed over in 1975 in good condition by the Council to a newly-established Harbour Company (now the Elie Harbour Trust), the harbour's future remains in local hands. Its present flourishing condition is an indication of the quality of their stewardship.

35. Firth of Forth - Map of 1645 by Gordon of Rothiemay

ANGVSIÆ PARS.

PART OF

ANGVS.

Arbroth

of

Tay

Inch-Ga

Divertie
Head

Tents-

Muirs.

Strath
kinnes

Sainct Andrews

Ardho-Neß

Kings-
Muir.

Fyfe-Neß

Keancrage Nooke

May Isle.

FORTHÆ ÆSTVARIVM

Scale approx. 2.4 miles to the inch

OF

FORTH

The Baß

Old Bastle

Gulan

North berwyck

North Berwick law

Tentallon

Seaton

Laß neß

Tinningham

RT   OF   LOTHI   AN   Dunbarr

Oriens

Appendix I

SIR JOHN ANSTRUTHER'S 1740 ROLL OF SHORE AND OTHER DUES+

Roll of the Customs, Shore Dues & Anchorages of Elie

The Shore Dues

	Inhabitants shall pay as under Sterling £ s d	Strangers shall pay as under Sterling £ s d
Wheat, Barley, Bear, pease, Oats, Rye		
Malt, Salt great or Small, Every Chalder	5_	6_
Meal – Every Chalder or 16 Bolls thereof	2_	5_
Salt – great or small, Every last thereof	3	4_
Barrels emptie, Every last yrof	1_	3
Herrings, Tar, Iron, Hemp or Taikle p last	5_	10_
Herrings exported Coastways Every 1000	1	2
Fresh Ditto unload from One Boat to another		
For Transportation p 1000	4	4
Fish of 18 Inches Length p 1000	8	16
Ditto of half Gadge p ditto	4	8
Ditto of Quarter Gadge p ditto	2	4
Lyme, Smiddie Coal - Chalder	3	6
Oyl & Soap p Last	18_	1 11_
Butter of Woolgrease p Barrel	1	2
Wine or Brandie p Tun	1 0	2 0
Beer p Chalder Bark p Tun	6_	1 1_
Kilp p Tun	4	8
English goods p Barrel Weight	1	2
Limons, Oranges, Raisens p Chist or Jar	1_	1_
Coal p Boll	–	2
Hydes p Dicker*	4	8
Botles p Groce 1 Botle or for every gross in money	1	1
Millstone, Bed, each shall pay offshore Dues	6_	6_
Runnerstone each shall pay by ways offshore		
Ditto h	5_	5_
Lintseed p hog	3	6
Ironstone for each tun shipped	–	1

Potatoes for every Hundred Bolls Three shillings & Six Pence Sterling
Or smaller quantitys in proportion

NOTES

Some of the measures used varied between districts and could be different for different commodities. On the river Forth a chalder of grain or meal would be about 30 hundredweight, 1_ tons, though the chalder was a measure not of weight but of volume, equal to 16 bolls. In modern terms a boll was approximately 36 gallons. A boll of oats weighed between 14 and 16 stones, depending on quality. A boll of wheat was only about 24 gallons, but would weigh rather more than a boll of oats.

The last was also a variable measure of volume. Judging by the rates for salt per chalder and per last the last used for salt seems to have been little over half a chalder. The use of two measures for salt suggests that the different producers and merchants used different measures, perhaps related to the size of the containers and carts they used.

The two rates for coal, by the chalder for "Smiddie Coal", and by the boll for other coal, indicate two qualities, inferior coal in bulk charged at a lower rate than that for coal for general use.

* A dicker was 10 hides, a measure which can be traced back to Roman times.

+ The original roll is in the possession of David Thomson.

Shore Dues continued

	Inhabitants shall pay as under Sterling £ s d	Strangers shall pay as under Sterling £ s d
DEAL Board, Trees Oak plank great or Small, Clapboard, Scows, Batton's Beds, Posts, Stings, Harrowbills, Oak Spokes Hoops, Staves, Sive rimbs, or other Wood Commodities; Also sclate, Tyle, Brick Earthen pots Can's, Peats or any other Commodities of that Nature or Qualitie ONE for every hundred or for the Timber the value thereof After the Kings Dutie is paid in place Of the said quantity & whereas it happens to be great Loggs of Timber which doth not Amount to hundreds Then the Same must be valued by two Indifferent Persons for each 100 pence of theyr value	1	1
Furniture landed from any Vessel or boat To pay one pennie sterling for the Barrel Bulk to Inhabitants and two pence sterling for Every Barrel Bulk to Strangers	1	2

Boats or other vessels selling dried fish
To pay for every twinty Fish one fish or the value thereof
The Teinds of Fishes or Herrings to be uplifted
For all Fish and Herrings Caught by the Elie
Fishers and Brought into the Elie Harbour
And there Sold or if Sold to Boats at Sea
To Pay to the Teind Master One Fish or One Herring
Every Ten Fish or Herrings

For all Fish and herrings Caught by the Elie
Fishers and Sold in other harbours or at
Distance from Elie One Fish or One Herring for
Every Twenty being Half Teind

For all Fish and Herrings caught by Stranger
Boats and Brought into Elie and there Sold
In Elie Harbour to Pay One Fish or One Herring
For every Twenty being Half Teind

Anchorage Duties

	Inhabitants shall pay as under Sterling			Strangers shall pay as under Sterling		
	£	s	d	£	s	d
Ships, Snows, Brigs, Sloops or other Vessels Shall pay for every Nett Tun		1			1	
Ships foreign or other vessels p Nett Tun		1_			1_	
Kinghorn, or other passage Boats		6			6	
Drave or Couper Boats during the fishing season		6_			6_	
Ditto every time they harbour in place yrof		2			2	
Small open Fishing Boats		2			2	
BOATS from 4 ot 8 Lasts Burden		4			4	

The Rule of Collecting the Anchorage in Elie
Harbour shall be by the Tuns mentioned in the
Register and every Shipmaster Shall be Obliged to
Produce his Register to the Shoarmaster to be the Rule
of Payment

	£	s	d	£	s	d
Vessells Belonging to Elie per Tun					1	
Coasting Vessells per Do		1			1	
English Vessells per Do		1			1	
Foreign Vessells per Do		1_			1_	

N.B. These was the Anchorage Dues in my Writing
Fixed by the late Deceased Old Sir John Anstruther
Baronet when the Elie shoar was Lett to John
Ovenstone Senr which is Attested by
      Robert. Maltman
Every Vessell that is Built in Elie
    Shall Pay of Dockmail to
      The Shoarmaster

	£	s	d	£	s	d
The Shoarmaster	5	0		10	0	

Anchorages Continued

Rules to be Observed by all Masters of
Vessells that comes to the Elie Harbour
That the Shoarmaster shall Direct the Proper
Births for the Vessells
And every Shipmaster Shall Slack his Ropes
When the Shoarmaster desires for the Accommodation
Of the other Vessells going out or coming
into the Harbour under the Penalty of Five
Pounds sterling for Disobeying
No Shipmaster to be Allowed to lay any
Anchors inhead without the Permission
Of the Shoarmaster otherways the Shipmaster
Shall be liable to the Damages to be
Determined, which the vessels comeing into
The Harbour mayReceive from Said Anchors
Also to the Penalty of Five Pounds Sterling
For Disobeying the Shoarmasters Orders
If the Shipmaster will not slack his Rope
After being desired by the Shoarmaster Once
Twice & Three Times after that If the
Shoarmaster Sees Occasion on Necessity he shall
Have liberty to Cast off the Said Ropes If it can
Be done, or if Not Cutt the Same If the Ship-
Master continues Obstinate and will not obey the
Shoarmasters Orders when vessels is comeing into
The Harbour or going out of the Harbour.

Toun Customs

	Inhabitants shall pay as under Sterling			Strangers shall pay as under Sterling		
	£	s	d	£	s	d
GOODS weighed Every Stone Shall pay			–			–
DITTO – For every Boardfull weighted			–			1
MEAL – Made from Wheat, Barley, Bear						
Oats, pease or Rye Sold in the Toun p Bag			2			2
TIMBER or other Mrchandize going out from						
The Toun p Wain or Cart			2_			2_
MALT - Every Bag thereof Sold in toun by						2
CART LOADS of Timber & drawn by 2 Horses			2			2
ONE HORSE Load of Ditto			–			–
BUTTER, Every Stone yrof brought to Toun for Sale			–			–
APPLES, pears or oyr fruit every load yrof for Ditto			2			2
MILLSTONE Bed every one carried from the Toun			6_			6_
RUNNER Stone everone Carried from Ditto			3_			3_
All Strangers comeing with Cloths of						
Different kinds, Including Ribbons						
Lawns & hardware Merchants	1	-	-			
Galligoes and Printed Cloths of every						
Kinds If the Sale Continues only						
One day to pay					1	6
If they Continue Two days 1/3 per day or					2	6
If they Continue longer than Two						
days then to pay for each day					1	-
during the time they stay						
The Officer not to Advertise the sale						
Of any Goods brought in until						
the Exposer has Satisfied, or Engaged						
to satisfy the Customer						
Every Cart with Stone Ware of Piggs						2
Every Cart with Pewter or Other hardware						2
For Each Sixteen Bolls of Grain brought						
Into the Toun of Elie in Carts and Putt						
Into Granary. If not Shipped but Sold						
The Same to pay Three Pence per Cart reccond						
Eight Bolls when going away or for						
The Sixteen Bolls being One Chalder						6

Appendix II

FIFESHIRE JOURNAL MAY 12 1836

Elie Harbour. The Subscribers being convinced that important benefits would accrue to the Agricultural Interests of the east Fife by the erection of a Low-Water Pier at Elie, to open up a direct communication with the London and Yorkshire Markets:- Request a Meeting with the Proprietors and Tenants of the District within the School-Room, Elie on Tuesday 17th inst, at One o'Clock, PM to consider the propriety of inviting Mr Stevenson, Civil Engineer to survey the Harbour of Elie, and ascertain at what expense the desired Low-Water-Pier can be constructed, and to adopt such measures at the Meeting may consider best calculated to accomplish the object in view.

Signed

WRK Douglas	Kenneth Hutchison
D Erskine	John Small
James Lindsay	John Cowie
James Lumsdaine	Philip Keddie
R A Anstruther	James Russell
John Dalyell	James Luke
H Randall Lt. RN	Robert Simpson
John Archibald	George Rogers
John Currie	John Wood
Arthur Gourlay	George Wood
William Henderson	David Carstairs
Andrew Beale	James Wyld
George Luke	

Elie 3D May 1836

Appendix III

A harbour or landing place erected about 14 chains within the tide mark of the village of Elie and on the margin of a small island, it consists of stone wall along the north and west side of the island and a Small Stone pier about 27 links long projecting at nearly a right angle from the forementioned wall *[Note: this is the wall on the north side of the Law, the "shore" built by Dishington and Scott about 1600]* along both of which *[i.e. the pier and the wall]* vessels can come for loading or unloading purposes, formerly a Breakwater of stone and lime erection connected to the South eastern end of the island with the main land affording a considerable shelter to the vessels in the harbour, but from neglect of Occasional Necessary Repairs this has been swept away piece-meal by the Action of the tide. Save a Small fragment close by this island. The pier and the other buildings forming the harbour are in an indifferent State of Repairs at present. It was once repaired by a general collection made at all the churches throughout the land. This was about the year 1696. It has 22 feet of water at springtides & is of easy access. The Chief Exports are Agricultural produce Fish & import goods for Shopkeepers and Merchants in the surrounding districts.

Sources and Bibliography

BOOKS

Ammianus Marcellinus, The Later Roman Empire: AD 354-378 (Penguin Translation), 1986

Anson, P., Fishing Boats and Fisher Folk on the East Coast of Scotland, 1930

Bower, W., Watt, D.E.R. (Ed) A History Book for Scots: Selections from the Scotochronicon (1440s), 1998

Breeze, D.J., The Northern Frontiers of Roman Britain, 1982

Bremner, D., The Industries of Scotland, 1869

Brodie, I., Steamers of the Forth, 1976

Bruce, W.S., The Railways of Fife, 1980

Burton, J.H., The History of Scotland (2nd Edition), 1897

Chambers, R. (Ed) and Thomson, T. (Ed), Biographical Dictionary of Eminent Scotsmen (Revised Edition),1875

Chapman, T., Handbook to Elie and East of Fife, (2nd Edition), 1892

Corstorphine, J.K., East of Thornton Junction: The Story of the Fife Coast Line

Dickinson, W.C., Donaldson, G., Milne, I.A. (Eds) A Source Book of Scottish History (Vols. II and III) 1953:1954

Dickson, J., Emeralds Chased in Gold: The Islands of the Forth, 1899

Dow, F.D., Cromwellian Scotland: 1651-1660, 1979

Ferrier, W.M., The North Berwick Story, 1980

Fyfe, J.G. (Ed), Scottish Diaries and Memoirs: 1550-1746, 1927

Geddie, J., The Fringes of Fife (2nd Edition), c.1924

Gibson, J.S., Playing the Scottish Card: The Franco-Jacobite Invasion of 1708, 1988

Gifford, J., The Buildings of Scotland: Fife, 1988

Heaton, P., Yachting: A History 1955

Keddie, H., Three Generations – The Story of a Middle Class Family: Extract published by the Society in "Growing up in Earlsferry" (Ed. Jim Bell) 2005

Kirk, R., St Andrews, 1954

Lamont, J., The Chronicle of Fife from 1649 to 1672, 1810

Lavery, B., Maritime Scotland, 2001

Leighton, J.M., History of the County of Fife, 1840

Lenman, B., The Jacobite Risings in Britain 1689-1746, 1980

Lethbridge, T.C., The Painted Men, 1954

Lyon, C.J., History of St. Andrews, 1843

Mackay, A.J.G., History of Fife and Kinross, 1896

Mathew, D., Scotland under Charles I, 1955

McWilliam, C., Scottish Townscape, 1975

Melville, J., The Historie of the Lyff of James Melvill (1556-1614) Extract printed in Fyfe, J.G., 1927

Millar, A.H., Fife, Pictorial and Historical, 1895

Nichols, D. (Ed), Intercepted Post August to December 1745, 1956

Nicoll, J., Diary for the years 1650-1667: Extracts printed in Fyfe, J.G., 1927

Pryde, G.S., A New History of Scotland (Vol. II), 1962

Sibbald, R., History and Description of Fife and Kinross, 1710

Smith, P., The Lammas Drave and the Winter Herrin', 1985

Smout, T.C., Scottish Trade on the Eve of the Union 1660-1707, 1963

Stevenson, D., The Scottish Revolution, 1973

Symon, J.A., Scottish Farming, Past and Present, 1959

Webb, W., Coastguard: An Official History

Wemyss, D., (2nd Earl 1610-1679) Diary Extract printed in Fyfe, J.G., 1927

Wilkie, J., The History of Fife, 1923

Wilkie, J., Bygone Fife, 1931

Wood, W., The East Neuk of Fife, 1887

Wyntoun, A., The Orygynal Cronykil of Scotland, C.1406 (Quoted in Chapman), 1892)

Yeoman, P., Pilgrimage in Medieval Scotland

The Statistical Account of Scotland (Sir John Sinclair, Ed): Kilconquhar 1793, Elie 1796

The New Statistical Account of Scotland, Vol. XIII 1837

The Third Statistical Account of Scotland, Fife, by Alexander Smith, 1952

JOURNALS, NEWSPAPERS AND OCCASIONAL PUBLICATIONS

Coull, J., The Role of the Fishery Board in the Development of Scottish Fishing Harbours c. 1809-1939, In Scottish Economic and Social History, Oct 15, 1995

Graham, A., Archaeological Notes on Some Harbours in Eastern Scotland, in the Proceedings of the Society of Antiquaries in Scotland, Vol. CI, Session 1968 – 69

Law, George., Articles on the North Berwick Ferry, in Scottish Historical Review, Vol.2, 1905

Mills, C.M., The Granary, Elie Harbour, Fife: a contribution to the development of dendrochronology in Scotland, in the Tayside Fife Archaeological Journal for 2002 (No.8)

East Fife Observer, 1914 – 1938

East Fife Record, 1857 – 1913

Fife Herald, 1847

Fifeshire Journal, 1836 – 1857

Morris, Ron, Aboard HMS May Island, 2004

UNPUBLISHED DOCUMENTS

The principal sources in this category are the following:-

A. The extensive archive of local documents, maps, plans, etc., collected and preserved by David Thomson and in his possession.

These include:-

1. Royal Charters and other documents of title, including copies and some originals;

2. a large bound volume containing a register of titles and other documents chiefly relating to Elie Estate properties, which were lodged with the Scottish Record Office in June 1961;

3. bound volumes of estate accounts and inventories;

4. documents relating to the Bill which became the Elie Harbour Act, 1857;

5. plans and contract documents relating to harbour works;

6. copies of Town Council minutes and other Council papers bearing on harbour affairs;

7. miscellaneous documents concerning the harbours of Elie Bay; and

8. manuscript notes of his own researches.

B. Documents in the care of the National Archives of Scotland (Scottish Record Office), which include:-

1. an extensive collection of Elie Estate papers dating from the reign of William the Lion (1165 – 1214) to the mid-19th C.;

2. Leith Custom House books;

3. East Fife Admiralty Court records;

4. Anstruther Registers of Shipping.

C. Documents in the care of St. Andrews University Library, including Earlsferry Town Council minutes 1806 – 1929; Elie Town Council minutes 1905 – 1929; and Elie and Earlsferry Town Council minutes 1929 – 1975.

Index